Anatomy
of the Soul

THE TEACHINGS OF KABBALAH SERIES

by Rabbi Yitzchak Ginsburgh

The Hebrew Letters
Channels of Creative Consciousness

The Mystery of Marriage
How to Find True Love and Happiness in Married Life

Awakening the Spark Within
Five Dynamics of Leadership that can Change the World

Transforming Darkness into Light
Kabbalah and Psychology

Rectifying the State of Israel
A Political Platform based on Kabbalah

Living in Divine Space
Kabbalah and Meditation

Body, Mind, and Soul
Kabbalah on Human Physiology, Disease, and Healing

Consciousness & Choice
Finding Your Soulmate

The Art of Education
Internalizing Ever-New Horizons

What You Need to Know About Kabbalah

Kabbalah and Meditation for the Nations

Anatomy of the Soul

A Sense of the Supernatural
Interpretation of Dreams and Paranormal Experiences

Anatomy
of the
Soul

Rabbi Yitzchak Ginsburgh

Prepared for publication
by Yechezkel Anis

SECOND EDITION

ג	ל	ע	י	נ	י
ו	א	ב	י	ט	ה
נ	פ	ל	א	ו	ת
מ	ת	ו	ר	ת	ד

Gal Einai

Jerusalem • New York • Los Angeles

The Teachings of Kabbalah Series

Anatomy of the Soul

Rabbi Yitzchak Ginsburgh

Prepared for Publication by Yechezkel Anis

Printed in the United States of America and Israel
Second Edition

For information:

Gal Einai
PO Box 1015
Kfar Chabad 72915
tel.: +972-3-9608008

email: ge@inner.org

Internet: www.inner.org

For orders:

email: books@inner.org

Internet: www.inner.org

Gal Einai produces and publishes books, pamphlets, and recorded lectures by Rabbi Yitzchak Ginsburgh. To receive a catalog of our products in English and/or Hebrew, please contact us at any of the above addresses, email ge@inner.org, or visit our website.

Text Layout: David Hillel

Cover Design: Shmuel Kaffe

ISBN: 978-965-7146-20-0

Table of Contents

Preface to the Second Edition

One of the most important contributions of Chasidut to Judaism has been in the realm of psychology. Chasidic teachings interpret and apply the myriad Kabbalistic metaphors to the realm of the human psyche and soul. Yet, for all the expansive analyses and discussion of the human psyche produced by the Chasidic masters (specifically the Rebbes of Chabad-Lubavitch), there has been a pronounced lack of an ordered and modern review of the psyche. As our modern society, including observant and even Chasidic Jews, has made consultation with psychologists a staple of life, this lack has become even more severe. Secularly trained psychologists or mental health practitioners approach the psyche from various different perspectives, which at best approximate its true nature and complexity.

In the early years of the 20th century, Dr. Fischel Schneersohn, a colleague of Sigmund Freud and a relative of the then Lubavitcher Rebbe, Rabbi Shalom Dov Ber Schneersohn, took it upon himself to translate the Chasidic nomenclature and discourse on the psyche into scientific language that would be useful to the modern psychologist. Unfortunately, for whatever the reasons may be, his yearning to share the Torah's wisdom on the psyche was not to be fulfilled. Since then, the need for introducing these teachings to the public in general and to the professional field of psychologists has only grown.

❧❧

This volume is a second edition of the 80-page pamphlet published in 1995 by the same name. That pamphlet was prepared by our dear friend Yechezkel Anis; it enjoyed tremendous popularity, and has been out-of-print for a number of years. Since the publication of the first edition, we have published another work on Chasidic Psychology titled *Transforming Darkness into Light: Kabbalah and Psychology*, which focuses on the use of a central teaching of Chasidut in dealing with anxiety. The present work, which is more structural and foundational, serves to complements it. We recommend accessing our website, **www.inner.org**, for more complementary material on this and related subjects.

Recently, we have published a greatly expanded and revised Hebrew text titled *Hanefesh* (The Psyche), which is in large part based upon the same model presented in this volume. It serves as the basic text for Gal Einai's Ba'al Shem Tov School for professional Chasidic psychology (located in Jerusalem).

The present volume contains some new material from *Hanefesh*, but is not exhaustive in that respect. We have also included a glossary and indexes in this edition. When the first edition of *The Anatomy of the Soul* was published, it was our editorial decision to refer to the various Kabbalistic and Chasidic terms such as the *sefirot* and their motivational inner aspects by their English transliteration (e.g., *chochmah* for wisdom and *bitul* for selflessness, etc.). Though in our recent works we have preferred using the English translation, we have not changed the original text in this respect. Whenever a verse that contains two Names of God is quoted, the essential Name, *Havayah* (יהוה) is referred to by a small-caps "GOD," while the second Name appears as "God." Hebrew words in bold print designate the numerical value (*gematria*) of the word in addition to the word itself; for example: יהוה designates both God's essential Name and its numerical value of 26).

In the future, we hope to publish a third edition of *The Anatomy of the Soul* with all of the content of *Hanefesh* plus additional material. May the Almighty grant us the opportunity to do so.

1

The Root
of the Soul

the root of the soul						
	powers	**transcendent**	pleasure	simple	faith (the simple song) (א)	
				composite	delight of intellect (the 2-part song) (ב)	
					delight of the emotions (the 3-part song) (ג)	
					delight of the speech (the 4-part song) (ד)	
			will	supreme	beyond reason and understanding (ה)	
				common	in accordance with reason and understanding (ו)	
		immanent	intellect	hidden	koa'ch hamaskil (ז)	
				revealed	chochmah (bitul) (ח)	binah (simchah) (ט)
					da'at (yichud) (י)	
			character attributes	arroused	chesed (ahavah) (כ)	gevurah (yirah) (ל)
					tiferet (rachamim) (מ)	
				innate	netzach (bitachon) (נ)	hod (temimut) (ס)
					yesod (emet) (ע)	
					malchut (shiflut) (פ)	
	garments		thought	focused thought	intelligent thought (צ)	
				random reflection	perpetual drift of thought (ק)	
			speech	profound	words spoken from the heart (ר)	
				superficial	words that issue only from the lips outward (ש)	
			action		equalizing great and small (ת)	

The Root of the Soul 1

The soul is man's spiritual bridge between his experience of the body and the physical world around him and his experience of God.

We learn this from one of the only extant writings of the Ba'al Shem Tov[1] himself, where he writes of three levels of consciousness called worlds, souls, and Divinity:

> ...in every letter there are Worlds, Souls, and Divinity, and they ascend, and connect, and unify with each other; and afterwards the letters connect and unify to become a word; and [then] unify in true unification in Divinity. Include your soul with them in each and every state. And, all the worlds unify as one and ascend to produce an infinitely great joy and pleasure...[2]

Thus, the consciousness of souls is an intermediate state that links the consciousness of worlds with that of Divinity.

The level of worlds includes both man's animal soul (נֶפֶשׁ הַבַּהֲמִית, *nefesh habahamit*) as well as his native, human intellect—called the intellectual soul (נֶפֶשׁ הַשִּׂכְלִית, *nefesh hasichlit*).[3] The level of souls comprises man's Divine soul (נֶפֶשׁ הָאֱלֹקִית, *nefesh ha'elokit*).[4,5]

The Intellectual Soul

In a seminal article[6] on the nature of the intellectual soul, the previous Lubavitcher Rebbe explains its unique role in bridging the animal and Divine souls:

> The Divine soul is mainly intellectual in nature. Even though it also contains emotions, its essence is intellectual... The animal soul is mainly emotional. Though it also contains intellect, this intellect serves the emotions by understanding what is good for it [the animal soul] and how to attain what it wants, i.e., physical wealth, belongings, honor, prestige, and the like. It also serves to intellectually self-legitimize one's conduct, not with arguments taken from Torah, but by arguments aimed at illustrating one's self-merit, etc...
>
> The essence of the animal soul is craving. Because it is from the lower parts of *nogah*,[7] its potency is enclothed in coarseness and therefore all of its desires and will focus on bodily needs...

But, the Supernal intent is that the animal soul be refined and purified, meaning that the power of craving in it be used to serve God—through the learning of Torah, the performance of the commandments, and in prayer, the toil of the heart... This refinement is achieved by the Divine soul.

[But, because] the Divine soul and the animal soul are opposites, an intermediate between the two is necessary and this intermediary is the intellectual soul. Though the intellectual soul is also from *nogah*, it is from the higher states of *nogah*, i.e., the intellect. And even though this intellect understands physical-natural concepts—e.g., knowing the breakdown of every material, all of its parts, their nature, etc., meaning that the knowledge focuses upon the somethingness of the object, not its nothingness—still, it is intellect and it is natural and thus connects the Divine soul with the animal soul.

With the help of the intellectual soul, the Divine soul clarifies and explains Divine concepts to the animal soul... [By doing so] the intellectual soul severs the animal soul from the evil inclination. Because the intellectual soul is intellect, albeit natural intellect [focusing on nature and the somethingness in nature, as above], its proclivity is to be drawn higher to that which is above it [i.e., the Divine soul]. For this reason, the intellectual soul is a vessel ready to receive insight from the intellect and emotions of the Divine soul and these insights are that which the intellectual soul can then clarify and explain to the animal soul.

The Intellect and Free Will

It follows therefore, that man's free will depends on his intellectual soul, because truly the only significant choice in life lies between following one's Divine soul and following the cravings of one's animal soul. This is indicated in the Torah in the verse that refers to free will: "…I have placed before you life and death, the blessing and the curse, and you shall choose life, so that you and your children shall live."[8] As the Alter Rebbe[9] writes:

> As it says, 'You shall choose life'… For choice is found in the intellect [the intellectual soul] alone—the choice for selecting the good and despising the evil… One must condition one's intellect to habitually choose life.[10]

Return to the Source

The level of souls allows man to existentially leap from the confines of worlds to the infinity of Divinity. This is so, for the apparently finite powers inherent in the soul reflect, paradoxically, the essentially infinite attributes of the Divine. Ultimately, the power of the soul is to reveal to the consciousness of worlds their intrinsic connection to Divinity—that every aspect and entity of creation reflects its Creator—and how, in essence, all is One.

By doing so, the soul is able to essentially leap backwards and uncover the objective existence of the Creator before He created the universe. Let us explain this point.

One of the deepest teachings of Chasidut[11] is that to bridge the gap between the Creator in and of Himself and creation, three quantum leaps are needed between four incommensurable ontological-psychological states.[12] The first leap is from the Creator in and of Himself to His Infinititude (specifically to the *sefirah* of kingdom of His Infinititude). The second leap is from His Infinititude to His effluent nature, the life-force within creation. The third leap is from His effluent nature to the reality of created worlds.

The three dimensions of Divinity, souls, and worlds are actually superseded by the Divine in and of Itself (Divinity, especially in Hebrew, implies a revelation of the Divine, not the Divine in and of Itself). Thus, there are actually four dimensions in this model. With this in mind, we can parallel these four dimensions to the four incommensurable ontological states involved in the creative process:

Creator in and of Himself	Divine in and of Itself
His Infinititude	Divinity
His effluence	Souls
Created worlds	Worlds

The corollary of this parallelism is that our own ascent from worlds to souls to Divinity and finally to the Divine Itself, is a reflection of the process of creation in reverse order.

The Magid of Mezritch was known to state that the actions of the *tzadikim*—those unique souls able to leap higher and higher until they reach the Divine Itself—are greater than the act of creation, because in creation, God transformed nothingness into somethingness. But, by their pursuit of Divinity, the *tzadikim* transform somethingness back into nothingness.[13]

Contemplating the Divine

Job, in his suffering, said, "From my flesh, I envision God."[14] This verse[15] is interpreted in *Chasidut* to mean that the way to "envision God"[16,17] is through the contemplation of one's own flesh, where "flesh" here represents the fabric of one's subjective experience.

The traditional approach of Kabbalah has been to interpret the term "flesh" in this verse as suggestive of a literal correspondence between the structure of man's body and the configuration of Divine forces that sustain Creation.[18] In contemplating such a correspondence, one must possess a mature and developed capacity for abstract thought if one is to avoid the risk of falling into dangerous substantiation of the Divine.

In his writings on prayer, the third Lubavitcher Rebbe writes:

> For this reason the Ba'al Shem Tov declared that Kabbalah texts should not be studied. Because, one who does not know how to abstract the physical language finds himself growing coarser by studying these texts, specifically when poorly imagining Divinity as it is revealed through its particularized aspects. Even though the

words of the Arizal are trustworthy and true...[19]

The Chasidic approach, aimed at avoiding such risk, has been to adopt the structure of the soul—its express functions and properties—as a more appropriate basis for reflecting upon the Divine.

Unlike the soul, Kabbalah considers the physical body to be a fallen entity in need of rectification. The background for this identification is the breaking of the vessels—a particular stage of the creative process during which the light (or, energy) emanated by the Creator through Primordial Man shattered the vessels in which it was contained. The broken vessels became affixed to the physical matter in creation and serve as its internal life-force,[20] but, because they are broken they must first be rectified in order that the body truly mirror the Divine.

Contrastingly, the soul did not follow the same path of descent into our reality and therefore was not affected like the body by the shattering of the vessels. The soul—i.e., the Divine soul—remains eternally bound to its Divine source and therefore mirrors Divinity in a pure and undistorted manner.[21] The primary contribution of *Chasidut* to the Jewish mystical tradition lies in this emphasis upon the correspondence between man's subjective experience and the nature of Divine reality. Whereas Kabbalah traditionally employs a highly technical terminology in constructing its anatomy, as it were, of the Divine, *Chasidut* humanizes the path to enlightenment by utilizing meaningful terms and analogies derived from the store of the soul.[22]

For this reason, the Chasidic interpretation of the term "flesh" in the above verse assumes it to be symbolic of not only one's physical state but primarily of one's spiritual condition. Such an assumption is supported by the verse:[23] "And I will remove the heart of stone from their flesh and will give them a heart of flesh." Here, the newly sensitized spirit with which man is to be endowed in Messianic times is referred to as a "heart of flesh." It comes to replace the "heart of stone" which presently dulls man to God's presence in the world.[24]

Thus, by virtue of the innate features—both material and spiritual—that characterize his particular being, man can approach the Divine enigma underlying Creation. Having been created "in the image of God,"[25] his own body and soul constitute a supreme analogue for understanding the Divinity upon which his very existence is modeled.

The soul, at its root, is conceived in Chasidic thought as an extension of God's infinite and transcendent being. As an actual "portion of God from above,"[26] the Divine soul of Israel attests to the existence of God by virtue of its very being.[27] When enclothed within a physical body, it continues to assert its Divine origin through the infinite variety of ways by which it negotiates the encounter with its corporeal self as well as with outer reality.

Our purpose here is to explore the structure of the soul as manifest through its various properties and functions. The accompanying diagram, which illustrates the individual powers of the soul and the channels by which they achieve expression, is entitled *Etz Hacha'im* (עֵץ הַחַיִּים, "The Tree of Life"). This name echoes the Kabbalistic conception of man's spirit as a multi-branched, yet unitary, source of eternal life, primordially rooted in the ground of God's supernal being.[28]

Psyche and Soul

Our sages teach us[29] that the soul is referred to in the Bible by five names, each of which reflects a different dimension of man's Divine character.

> By five names it [the soul] is called: *nefesh* (נֶפֶשׁ, psyche), *ruach* (רוּחַ, spirit), *neshamah* (נְשָׁמָה, soul), *chayah* (חַיָּה, living one), and *yechidah* (יְחִידָה, singular one).[30]

In Hebrew, the collective noun "soul," is used to refer to all five levels. Throughout our current study of the soul, whenever we use the word soul, we are actually referring to the *nefesh*, or the psyche.[31] Thus, in the anatomical diagram that we will be studying, the left-most column — "the root of the soul" — actually refers to the root of the psyche.

Because of the holographic (or, inter-inclusive) nature of the soul, all five levels of the collective soul are represented in it. In particular, the *yechidah* corresponds to pleasure, *chayah* corresponds to will, *neshamah* corresponds to the intellect, *ru'ach* corresponds to the character attributes, and *nefesh* corresponds to the garments, while the root of the *nefesh* is found already in the lowest of the character attributes, *malchut*.

Just as the holographic nature allows us to find all five levels in the *nefesh*, so it implies that in parallel to our diagram, four other diagrams are possible, each depicting the (similar) anatomy of the other four levels. In each of these diagrams, the left-most column would indicate the root of each of the four other levels of the soul. As our purpose for the moment is to gain the broadest possible understanding of the spiritual dynamic governing our inner lives, we will proceed to examine the anatomy of the soul in terms of the *nefesh*, or psyche.[32]

the root of the soul	powers	transcendent	*yechidah* (pleasure)	simple	faith (the simple song) (א)	
				composite	delight of intellect (the 2-part song) (ב)	
					delight of the emotions (the 3-part song) (ג)	
					delight of the speech (the 4-part song) (ד)	
			chayah (will)	supreme	beyond reason and understanding (ה)	
				common	in accordance with reason and understanding (ו)	
		immanent	*neshamah* (intellect)	hidden	koa'ch hamaskil (ז)	
				revealed	chochmah (bitul) (ח)	binah (simchah) (ט)
					da'at (yichud) (י)	
			ru'ach (character attributes)	arroused	chesed (ahavah) (כ)	gevurah (yirah) (ל)
					tiferet (rachamim) (מ)	
				innate	netzach (bitachon) (נ)	hod (temimut) (ס)
					yesod (emet) (ע)	
					nefesh (the root of all the garments) malchut (shiflut) (פ)	
	garments		thought	focused thought	intelligent thought (צ)	
				random reflection	perpetual drift of thought (ק)	
			speech	profound	words spoken from the heart (ר)	
				superficial	words that issue only from the lips outward (ש)	
			action		equalizing great and small (ת)	

Notes:

1. The Ba'al Shem Tov (1698-1760) was the founder of the Jewish renewal movement known as Chasidut. For more, see our upcoming multi-volume series *The Torch of Israel*.

2. *Keter Shem Tov*, 1. See also the introduction to *The Hebrew Letters*.

3. The animal soul is discussed in the second half of the first chapter of *Tanya*. The intellectual soul is mentioned in the foreword to the second part of the *Tanya* and discussed in greater length in the writings of Reb Hillel of Paritsch.

4. The Divine Soul is discussed in length in the *Tanya*, beginning with chapter 2.

5. All human beings posses a Divine *spark*. However, only in the Jewish people, the descendants of Abraham, Isaac, and Jacob, has this spark been integrated into their psyche and manifests itself as a *soul*—the Divine soul. For the non-Jew, the Divine spark continuously hovers above the psyche. For more see *Kabbalah and Meditation for the Nations*, pp. 55ff.

6. *"Chaveev Adam"* in *Sefer Hama'amarim 5700*, pp. 95ff.

7. *Nogah* is the intermediate *klipah*, or state of being, that lies between the pure and the impure. See *Tanya*, chapters 6-8.

8. Deuteronomy 30:19.

9. The Alter Rebbe (The Elder Rebbe), Shne'ur Zalman of

Liadi (1745-1813) was the founder of the Chabad branch of Chasidut. His two most famous works are the *Tanya* and his updated *Shulchan Aruch*.

10. *Likutei Torah, Nitzavim* 46b-c. For a deeper explanation of this point, see *Ma'amarei Admor Ha'emtza'ee Devarim* v. 3, pp. 831-5.

11. Based on a passage in the *Zohar's* introduction (I, 15a) that begins with the words *"bereish hormanuta demalka."*

12. See also in length in our Hebrew volume, *Sod Hashem Liyerei'av*, pp. 188ff.

13. *Magid Devarav Leya'akov*, 11.

14. Job 19:26.

15. There are differing opinions among the commentators as to the literal meaning of this verse. Some see it, as we have suggested, as an expression of the positive impact that suffering and travail can have upon one's spiritual consciousness (see *Rashi ad loc.*). According to others, such as the *Targum*, Job's intention here is to state the opposite: only when his flesh becomes healed, will he once more be able to "envision God"—implying, as Maimonides explicitly points out (*Hilchot De'ot* 4:1), that a healthy body is a prerequisite to pursuing proper knowledge of God.

The apparent conflict between these two interpretations is resolved in *Chasidut* by suggesting that there exist two modes of enlightenment which derive from differing life-circumstances. The kind of insight which is only achievable by one of sound body is that which relates to God's "immanence," i.e. implicit presence within the rectified realm of material Creation. The "transcendent" aspect of His being, emanating from beyond the physical realm altogether, can only be intuited by one who manages to transcend the body through either ordeal and tribulation, as in the case of Job, or—more ideally—through the willing subjugation of his earthly nature to the discipline of Divine service prescribed by the Torah.

Another way that *Chasidut* approaches our verse from Job is by interpreting the words "from my flesh" as indicative of the need to focus upon one's mortality in order to achieve the degree of humility or "lowliness" (שפלות) that merits one the awareness of God's essential exaltedness. True lowliness, which is initially cultivated through simple fear of God, allows one to see beyond the immediate demands of his earthly existence so as to attain a spiritual elevation that transforms this simple fear into a mature awe of Divine singularity.

16. In this verse, the Hebrew word for "I shall envision" is אחזה. As opposed to its synonym, "I shall see" (אראה), which denotes direct, physical vision, this word (אחזה) implies prophetic, spiritual, and (usually) indirect vision viewed through the lens of a material or spiritual parable. In this case, the parable through which the vision is seen is the human flesh, whether in the sense of body or of soul. Significantly, this word's grammatical root in Hebrew is חזה, which, as a noun, means "chest." In Kabbalah, the chest is considered the seat of the spiritual eye of the heart (the heart of flesh, as will be explained).

17. The Hebrew word for "I shall envision" is אחזה and it appears only four times in the Bible. Two of those appearances are found in these verses from Job, which

in read: "From my flesh, *I envision* God; whom *I envision* myself, my eyes having seen and no others'" (Job 19:26-27).

Contemplating the five words connecting and including these two appearances of the word אחזה

‏"אחזה א־לוה. אשר אני אחזה"

one immediately notices that all of them begin with the letter *alef* (א), the first letter of the Hebrew alphabet whose form symbolizes the Divine image in which God created man. The numerical value of the five final letters ה י ר ה ה is 225, which means that their average value is 45, the *gematria* of "man" (אדם), stressing that man's flesh is indeed the subject of contemplation that reveals the Divine.

Furthermore, the first, middle, and last words taken together read אחזה ...אשר ...אחזה, meaning, "I shall envision... that which... I shall envision." We are immediately struck by the resemblance that this phrase bears with God's declaration at the burning bush: אהי־ה אשר אהי־ה, meaning, "I shall be that which I shall be" (Exodus 3:14). As the way in which God identified Himself before the people He was about to redeem from Egypt, these three words have come to represent the Divine Name of redemption for all time (see *Rashi ad loc.*). The idea that they express is similar to that intimated by the corresponding phraseology in Job: that God's existence is as self-verifying as one's own.

As if to reinforce the identification between these two Scriptural expressions, we find that the two words אהי־ה ("I shall be") and אחזה ("I shall envision") exactly equal each other in *gematria*—both possessing the numerical value of 21.

One of the Kabbalistic secrets connected with the Name אהי־ה אשר אהי־ה derives from the multiplication of the first אהי־ה by the second: 21 times 21 is equal to 441, the numerical value of the word אמת ("truth")—once again hinting at the intrinsic validation of God's being. Similarly the words א־לוה ("God") and אני ("myself"), which fill out the identified text-string of five words in Job and represent the merging poles of his vision, add up to אמת (441) when each letter is spelled out in full. The Name א־לוה itself is equal to 42, two times 21 (אחזה) as well.

18. See the introduction to *Tikunei Zohar*: "*Chesed* is the right arm and *gevurah* is the left," *et al.*

19. *Derech Mitzvotecha, Shoresh Mitzvat Hatefilah.*

20. This life-force is identical with the animal soul (and its intellectual aspect—the intellectual soul), which are tied intrinsically into the very essence of the physical body, sustaining it, not only as a living being, but tying its sub-atomic particles together into atoms, its atoms into molecules, its molecules into cells, and so on.

21. Even in a Jew (see note 5, above), at birth, the Divine soul is merely a spark enclothed within the animal soul. Therefore, the Divine soul remains in a state of separation from its Divine source until awakened, matured, and consciously connected to its source through the study of Torah. Unlike the Divine soul, the Torah is a ray (in contrast to a spark) of Divine light that is always connected consciously to its source in the Divine.

22. This added dimension of enlightenment, revealed through the teachings of *Chasidut*, led Rabbi Shmuel of

Lubavitch to expand upon a Zoharic reference by stating that while the early mystical tradition indeed represents the "soul of the *Torah*," *Chasidut* is "the soul of the soul of the Torah."

23. Ezekiel 11:19.

24. Highlighted in this verse is the implicit association between the root בשר, ("flesh") and the word בשורה ("future tiding," specifically the tiding of redemption).

25. Genesis 9:1.

26. Paraphrased from the verse: "And what might be my portion from God above and my inheritance from the Lord on high?" (Job 31:2). See *Tanya*, chapter 2. The adjective "actual" (*mamash*, in Hebrew) was first added by the 17th century Kabbalist, Rabbi Shabtai Sheftel, the author of *Shefa Tal*, in his volume titled *"Nishmat Shabtai."*

27. The root of the soul is identified in *Chasidut* with *emunah*—absolute faith in God's Being. Here, *emunah* is not meant to indicate, as elaborated later on, a capacity of the soul (see *Reshimot* #9 of the Lubavitcher Rebbe), but rather an axiomatic state of being that derives from the soul's grounding in Divine essence.

28. The image of the *Etz Hacha'im* is primarily employed in Kabbalah as a symbol for the evolution (השתלשלות) of created realms leading to our physical world. In both cases, the "tree" envisioned has roots in heaven and branches out, as it were, earthward—thus forming an inversion of its analogue in nature.

29. *Breisheet Rabbah* 14:11.

30. Each of these levels can actually be viewed as corresponding to a different property, or set of properties, appearing in our diagram. The

superconscious powers of pleasure and will correspond respectively to those strata of one's soul most sensitive to Divinity—*yechidah* (singular one) and *chayah* (living one). The conscious powers that comprise one's intellect and primary emotions correspond to the intermediate levels of *neshamah* (soul) and *ru'ach* (spirit). Finally, the powers that govern behavior, beginning with the *malchut* of the innate character attributes and including all of the garments are linked to the dimension of one's soul furthest removed from Divine awareness—the *nefesh* (psyche).

31. The two terms generally used to denote "soul" in the Hebrew vernacular are *nefesh* and *neshamah*. If one were to distinguish between them, one would say that the more common term—*nefesh*—describes the soul as enclothed within a body, while the more refined designation of *neshamah* describes the soul in terms of its pristine roots beyond the physical realm.

32. It should be further pointed out that the present exposition follows only one "view" of the "unfolding" process of the anatomy of the soul, the "horizontal" conceptualization of the soul "branching out" into the two equal realms of powers and garments, their subsequent subdivisions, etc. The "vertical" view sees the soul as first emanating its powers from its inner essence, "entering" into them as does "spirit" into body, and only then "creating" the garments in which to enclothe itself, as does body in clothing. The former, "abstract" view reflects the soul's level of "inspiration" (השראה) with regard to its lower manifestations, while the latter depicts its "envestiture" (התלבשות) into them. *Cf. Torah Or*, p. 13c *ff.*

2

Powers
and Garments

the root of the soul

powers	**transcendent**	pleasure	simple	faith (the simple song) (א)
			composite	delight of intellect (the 2-part song) (ב)
				delight of the emotions (the 3-part song) (ג)
				delight of the speech (the 4-part song) (ד)
		will	supreme	beyond reason and understanding (ה)
			common	in accordance with reason and understanding (ו)

immanent	intellect	hidden	koa'ch hamaskil (ז)
		revealed	chochmah (bitul) (ח) · binah (simchah) (ט)
			da'at (yichud) (י)
	character attributes	arroused	chesed (ahavah) (כ) · gevurah (yirah) (ל)
			tiferet (rachamim) (מ)
		innate	netzach (bitachon) (נ) · hod (temimut) (ס)
			yesod (emet) (ע)
			malchut (shiflut) (פ)

garments	thought	focused thought	intelligent thought (צ)
		random reflection	perpetual drift of thought (ק)
	speech	profound	words spoken from the heart (ר)
		superficial	words that issue only from the lips outward (ש)
	action		equalizing great and small (ת)

Powers and Garments

2

The first sub-division of the soul is into its "essential **powers**" or "properties" (כֹּחוֹת, *kochot*) and "**garments**" (לְבוּשִׁים, *levushim*), the expressive modes of thought, speech, and action in which the powers "enclothe" themselves as they become manifest to oneself and others. One can envision the powers as the hidden components of man's essence, while the garments are the means of expression which provide that essence with objective form.[1]

This distinction between essence and form is expressed as well in the creation of Adam and Eve, whereby God takes the initial and singular "living soul" of man[2] and confers on it two independent gender identities. The male Adam represents the abstract potential within man's essential powers while his female "help-mate"[3] Eve represents the expressive garments that help this potential attain concrete form.[4]

Another way of demonstrating this correspondence is by way of analogy to the Biblical figures of Jacob and his four wives. Jacob, whom the Talmud[5] tells us possessed beauty similar to that of Adam, serves as a symbol of the full spectrum of powers within man's soul. His four wives represent the various means of expression by which the powers achieve outer revelation. Leah and Rachel exemplify the garments of thought and speech, respectively, as expounded in *Chasidut*.[6] Zilpah and Bilhah, the wives who were also their half sisters' handmaidens, personify the mode of physical action as it follows either the dictates of thought, (Zilpah, Leah's handmaiden) or speech (Bilhah, Rachel's handmaiden).

powers	Essence	Adam	Jacob	
garments	Form	Eve	Leah	thought
			Rachel	speech
			Zilpah	action directed by thought
			Bilhah	action directed by speech

The duality of essence and form, associated with the distribution of powers and garments in the soul, is reflected as well in the two fundamental dialectics of Creation identified in *Chasidut* as "concealment and revelation" (וְגִלּוּי הֶעְלֵם, *he'elem vegilui*) and "concentration and expansion" (עֶצֶם וְהִתְפַּשְּׁטוּת, *etzem vehitpashtut*). These two dynamics achieve poetic expression through the image of the **chashmal** (חַשְׁמַל, the "electrum" found in Ezekiel's mystical vision of the heavenly chariot[7]). The *chashmal* appears in the verse as a band of energy or light surrounding the Divine figure seated on the heavenly throne. The Talmud[8] interprets it as a compound word, *chash-mal*, denoting a group of angels that "at times are silent [*chash*] and at times speak [*mal*]."

The spiritual energies of silence and speech—*chash* and *mal*[9]—suggest the dialectic of essence and form intimated through the powers and garments of the soul. The powers, existing in silent potential, dwell in a state of essential concealment identifiable with the state of *chash*. The revelation of these powers through the aegis of the garments advances the soul into a corresponding state of *mal*, serving as a paradigm for all forms of self-expression. The soul moves in perpetual oscillation between these two states of *chash* and *mal*—between hiddenness and revelation, concentration and expansion.[10]

essence	*Chash*	concealment	concentration
form	*Mal*	revelation	expansion

The Baal Shem Tov[11] treats the secret of the *chashmal* as a basic model for one's service of God. He describes how every act of Divine service proceeds in three stages: **submission** (הַכְנָעָה, *hachna'ah*), **separation** (הַבְדָּלָה, *havdalah*), and **sweetening** (הַמְתָּקָה, *hamtakah*).

Submission, corresponding to the state of *chash* in one's soul, is the submissive posture of silent subservience to God that one assumes upon realizing the great distance that separates him from the Divine. Submission helps one subdue the clamor of his ego, so that the sacred silence of his Divine soul can be restored.

Separation is the actual process of distinguishing between that which in oneself is sacred and that which is profane. Its culmination is the complete discarding of the outer layers of one's ego and laying bare the essential goodness at the core of the self. Hinted at as well by the root *mal*—this time, through its additional connotation of *milah* ("circumcision")— separation is the process whereby we remove the shell of indifference that dulls our sensitivity to God's presence in the world.

This stage is not explicitly identified in our above interpretation of the word *chashmal* since it is a transitional phase in the movement from silence to speech, containing elements of both. By virtue of its final subjugation of the ego, it culminates the service of *chash*; through exposing the essential virtue at the core of one's soul, it introduces the revelatory force of *mal* identified with speech—the latter achieving its greatest expression through the final phase of Divine service, sweetening.[12]

Sweetening derives from the primary force of *mal* in the soul. It represents the soul's capacity to outwardly express the genuinely pure dispositions that occupy the hidden center of one's mind and heart. Speech, particularly words of Torah and prayer, provides the perfect vehicle for substantiating the Divine light within one's soul. For in speech, more so than in any other human function, it is possible to experience oneself (once having passed through the first two stages of submission and separation) as a virtual conduit for Divinity. This stage is called "sweetening" because it implies the process referred to in Kabbalah as the "sweetening of severe judgments" (הַמְתָּקַת הַדִּינִים, *hamtakat hadinim*). By "sweetening," one converts negativity and conflict into a positive and constructive force by revealing the Divine Spark of good inherent in all being.

chash	Silence	submission	suppression of evil
mal (1)	circumcision	separation	separation of good from evil
mal (2)	Speech	sweetening	revelation of the good inherent in all

A symbolic representation of these three stages of Divine service can be found in the Biblical account of the first day of Creation. We are taught that at the outset of the day, immediately following the creation of the first light, light and darkness were intermingled. Only subsequently does the Torah state that they were separated one from the other and each was consigned to its own domain, the light to day and the darkness to night. Their initial enmeshment, however, produced the fundamental turbulence that lies at the heart of all evil and misery in Creation.

chash	Silence	mixture of light and darkness
mal (1)	circumcision	separating of light and darkness, day and night
mal (2)	Speech	evening and morning unite to become "one day"

The self, endowed with its own admixture of darkness and light, of the profane and the Divine, must seek to quell this turbulence through submission, so that ultimately the Divine soul can free itself from the influence of unrectified ego and assert itself supremely. This inner separation, prefigured in the primordial separation between light and darkness, day and night, allows one ultimately to experience his existence as unified and integrated—albeit possessed of apparently contrasting ingredients: "And there was evening and there was morning, [yet it was all] one day"—the darkness (of evening) and the light (of morning) together shine (as one day). This is the true objective of God in creation, the state of sweetening.[13]

Notes:

1. The idea of a simple, undifferentiated reality evolving
   into independent realms of essence and form is actually
   intimated in the very first verse of the Torah: "In the
   beginning God created the heavens and the earth
   [את השמים ואת הארץ]." The initial seed of Creation
   (represented by the abstract term את in the verse — see
   Kedushat Levi ad loc.) develops into the two fundamental
   spheres of heaven (essence) and earth (form).

   In Kabbalah, "essence" is associated with the world of
   Atzilut ("Emanation"), the first of the four created
   realms to descend out of God's primordial and
   exclusive being. At the level of *Atzilut*, God's "essential
   nature" is revealed in all its raw abstraction. Only with
   the succeeding realms of *Beriah* (*in potentia*
   "Creation" — formless matter), *Yetzirah* (spiritual
   "Formation" — generic "forms"), and *Asiyah* (physical-
   directed "Action" — individual entities) does that
   essence begin "enclothing" itself within progressively
   more expressive form, until it becomes completely
   masked by the physical world.

the creative process	creation of the world	worlds	referent in soul	
undifferentiated reality	the initial seed of creation		the root of the soul	
essence	the heavens	*Atzilut*	pow-ers	
form	the earth	*Beriah* *Yetzirah* *Asiyah*	gar-ments	thought
				speech
				action

2. Genesis 2:7, 19. This initial and undifferentiated force of
    "living soul" can be viewed as the actual "portion of
    God from above" which the Almighty contributed to
    the formation of mankind in symbolic "partnership"
    with Adam and Eve—the "parents" of mankind who
    represent the split in identity between powers and
    garments. This idea reflects the Talmudic adage that
    "there exist three 'partners' in [the conception of] man:
    his father and mother [who contribute the biological
    properties to their offspring] and the Holy One, blessed
    be He [who contributes man's 'living soul']." The
    paradigm we have identified with Creation—whereby
    initial reality "splits" into essence and form—can
    likewise be seen as a conceptual restatement of this
    homily, with God contributing the nuclear reality that
    is shaped into male essence (the heavens) and female
    form (the earth).

initial reality	nuclear reality	living soul	root of the soul
essence	the heavens	Adam	powers
form	the earth	Eve	garments

Another way of identifying the respective contributions
of God and man to the propagation of new life can be
formulated in terms of the Kabbalistic distinction
between "lights" (אורות) and "vessels" (כלים). God is the
ongoing source of "light" within Creation—a metaphor
for the essential soul-force enlivening its every aspect.

The powers and garments that we identify with this energy can be thought of as the respective male and female "vessels" by which Divine light takes on a particular character and hue. The male vessels enclothe the Divine light itself, whereas the female vessels enclothe—give expression and form to—the male vessels.

Lights	essential soul-force
male vessels	powers
female vessels	garments

3. Genesis 2:18.

4. This correspondence is most evident in Eve's name, Chavah (חוה), whose root literally means "to express outwardly." Adam's name (אדם), by virtue of its association with the opposing root, (דום) "silence", alludes to the realm of unarticulated potential with which he is identified. (See the following section on the relationship between silence and speech.)

   To the extent that Adam and Eve embody these contrasting domains within the soul, they can also be thought of as respectively representing the Divine "image" (צלם) and "likeness" (דמות) initially imprinted upon man's being. Man's Divine image, the abstract Divine potential engraved within his soul, is modeled through the "male" powers; while his Divine likeness, or tangible resemblance to God, is expressed through the "female" garments that endow that image with form.

Powers	Adam	Divine image
Garments	Eve	Divine likeness

5. *Bava Metzia* 84a.

6. *Torah Or, Vayeitzei* 22d-23b. See also our Hebrew article *"Cheit Hameragleem Veteshuvato"* (pp. 181-3) in *Rucho Shel Mashi'ach.*

7. Ezekiel 1:4, 27.

8. *Chagigah* 3b, in the opinion of the *braita* quoted there.

9. Both these roots are independently found in the Bible as well: The root *chash*, for example, appears in the expression "a time to be silent [ולחשות]" (Ecclesiastes 3:7), where it indicates the power to conceal that which one feels should not be revealed. (The related word חשאי actually possesses the connotation of both silence and secrecy.) The root *mal*, denoting speech, appears in numerous places throughout Scripture, including: "Who related [מלל] to Abraham..." (Genesis 21:7) and "Who can relate [ימלל] all of God's mighty deeds..." (Psalms 106:2).

10. The secret of the *chashmal* can actually be understood in varying contexts. In its most basic form, it expresses the paradoxical nature of Divine Being within the sublime world of *Atzilut* ("Emanation"). There, the opposing states of *chash* and *mal* exist simultaneously—thereby casting God's essence beyond all logical frames of reference.

In addition to the interpretation of *chashmal* as alternating states of silence and speech, Rav Yehudah

(*Chagigah, loc. cit.*) views the word as an abbreviation for חיות אש ממללות "the speaking angels of fire." These two interpretations correspond to the two dialectics of Creation referred to in our text: The first reflects the dialectic of concealment and revelation (העלם וגילוי). The second reflects the dialectic of concentration and expansion (עצם והתפשטות), insofar as the "angels of fire" represent concentrated spiritual energy that exists in an ongoing state of expansion (speech).

interpretations of chashmal	dialectics of creation
silence and speech	concealment and revelation
speaking angels of fire	contraction and expansion

11. *Keter Shem Tov* (ed. *Kehot*) 28.
12. The two elements of *havdalah*—removing the vulgar and revealing the good—are themselves reflected in the stages of circumcision: The first stage (מילה) involves cutting off the foreskin (ערלה), symbol of spiritual insensitivity; the second stage (פריעה), whereby the remaining transparent membrane is removed so as to expose the crown of the organ, symbolizes the revelation of the essential goodness within one's soul.
13. See *Tanya*, chapter 28, for further discussion of this topic.

3

Transcendent and Immanent Powers

the root of the soul						
powers	transcendent	pleasure	simple	faith (the simple song) (א)		
			composite	delight of intellect (the 2-part song) (ב)		
				delight of the emotions (the 3-part song) (ג)		
				delight of the speech (the 4-part song) (ד)		
		will	supreme	beyond reason and understanding (ה)		
			common	in accordance with reason and understanding (ו)		
	immanent	intellect	hidden	koa'ch hamaskil (ז)		
			revealed	chochmah (bitul) (ח)	binah (simchah) (ט)	
				da'at (yichud) (י)		
		character attributes	arroused	chesed (ahavah) (כ)	gevurah (yirah) (ל)	
				tiferet (rachamim) (מ)		
			innate	netzach (bitachon) (נ)	hod (temimut) (ס)	
				yesod (emet) (ע)		
				malchut (shiflut) (פ)		
garments		thought	focused thought	intelligent thought (צ)		
			random reflection	perpetual drift of thought (ק)		
		speech	profound	words spoken from the heart (ר)		
			superficial	words that issue only from the lips outward (ש)		
		action		equalizing great and small (ת)		

Transcendent and Immanent Powers

3

The expanded dynamic of *chash-mal-mal*, the Ba'al Shem Tov's three-phase model of Divine service, will help us understand the next stage of differentiation within the soul whereby the powers subdivide into the **surrounding powers** of the superconscious (מַקִיפִּים, *makifim*), and the **internal powers** (פְּנִימִיִּים, *pnimi'im*) of intellect and emotion identified with conscious experience. Together with the garments, there now appear three major branches within the structure of the soul.

The first class of powers, the surrounding ones, best express the silent and abstract state of *chash* which we have identified as characteristic of the powers as a whole. The internal ones, on the other hand, point to the state of *mal* present within the powers as well—the preliminary *mal* identified with "circumcision" and expressed through the service of separation.

As comprising one's varied intellectual and emotive capacities, the internal powers exhibit a greater degree of innate individuality and separation than the transcendent surrounding powers. Yet even though their disposition toward conscious expression suggests the influence of the *mal*-force in one's soul, the fact that the internal powers remain merely points of potential renders them much less expressive of that force than the garments of thought, speech, and action. The garments actually enable one's powers to achieve outer expression.[1]

The division between surrounding and internal powers in the soul reflects a corresponding distinction often made in Jewish thought between the conceptual categories of the general or universal (כְּלָל, *klal*) and the particular (פְּרָט, *perat*). A broad, universalistic attitude suggests the relative dominance of the surrounding powers in one's soul, while a consistently focused concern with individual detail implies the ascendant influence of the internal powers.

We will next show how these three fundamental branches of the soul—the surrounding powers, the internal powers, and the garments—divide into seven basic categories of experience from which all the overt properties of one's soul derive.

Notes:

1. Although our discussion has thus far focused upon the correspondence between *chashmal* and the duality of

powers and garments, one could just as easily identify the complete dynamic of *chashmal* within the powers alone: The element of *chash* would once again correspond to the transcendent, surrounding powers; however, the two levels of *mal* would be seen as corresponding to the sub-realms of intellect (reflecting the lesser state of *mal*) and emotion (expressing the dominant state of *mal*) subsumed within the inner powers alone.

On an even more fundamental plane, the principle of *chash-mal-mal* can be used to explain the relationship of both powers and garments to the initial undifferentiated soul-root from which they both split. This root can be thought of as representing the ultimate state of *chash* in the soul, while the powers and garments would correspond to the increasingly more dominant states of *mal* that the soul assumes in moving further toward outer experience and expression.

	soul as a whole	powers alone	powers and garments
chash	soul-root	superconscious powers	superconscious powers
mal (1)	powers	intellect	intellect and emotion
mal (2)	garments	emotion	garments

4

The Seven
Main Branches
of Inner Experience

And Their Manifestation as
Thirteen Measures
of Inner Experience

the root of the soul

powers / garments	transcendent / immanent	pleasure / will / intellect / character attribute / thought / speech / action	sub	content
powers	transcendent	pleasure	simple	faith (the simple song) (א)
			composite	delight of intellect (the 2-part song) (ב)
				delight of the emotions (the 3-part song) (ג)
				delight of the speech (the 4-part song) (ד)
		will	supreme	beyond reason and understanding (ה)
			common	in accordance with reason and understanding (ו)
	immanent	intellect	hidden	koa'ch hamaskil (ז)
			revealed	chochmah (bitul) (ח) binah (simchah) (ט)
				da'at (yichud) (י)
		character attribute	arroused	chesed (ahavah) (כ) gevurah (yirah) (ל)
				tiferet (rachamim) (מ)
			innate	netzach (bitachon) (נ) hod (temimut) (ס)
				yesod (emet) (ע)
				malchut (shiflut) (פ)
garments		thought	focused thought	intelligent thought (צ)
			random reflection	perpetual drift of thought (ק)
		speech	profound	words spoken from the heart (ר)
			superficial	words that issue only from the lips outward (ש)
		action		equalizing great and small (ת)

The Seven Main Branches
of Inner Experience

4

And Their Manifestation as
Thirteen Measures of Inner Experience

Both the surrounding and the internal powers identified above subdivide into two underlying ways of approaching reality. Together with the three basic modes of self-expression—the garments—we arrive at seven major branches of inner-experience:

surrounding powers:	1) super-conscious pleasure
	2) super-conscious will
internal powers:	3) conscious intellect
	4) conscious character-attributes
garments:	5) thought
	6) speech
	7) action

Inasmuch as the first six of these categories each possess dual aspects, there are altogether thirteen distinct "measures of experience" which the soul employs in probing reality. Let us now explore these in more detail.

Pleasure and Will

The transcendent powers of the soul—the *makifim*—are identified in *Chassidut* as the powers of superconscious **pleasure** (עֹנֶג, *oneg*) and **will** (רָצוֹן, *ratzon*). Every process within the soul begins with these two categories of experience. Though themselves beyond the grasp of reason, the powers of pleasure and will nevertheless exert a definite influence upon consciousness, albeit in an indirect and circuitous manner.

Intentional will, the initial force to assert itself in conscious life, is generally inspired by a deeper, more inscrutable will, which we have referred to as superconscious will. This most basic of drives powering our conscious existence is itself inspired by an even profounder force, the superconscious pleasure which guides the soul toward the pursuit of self-actualizing, outer-directed experience.[1]

Ultimately, the supreme state of the superconscious pleasure in the soul is that of **simple pleasure** (עֹנֶג פָּשׁוּט, *oneg pashut*), the completely abstract and unstructured superconscious sensation which derives from the soul's experiencing its source in the Divine. A subsequent form of pleasure, **composite pleasure** (עֹנֶג

מֶרְכָּב, *oneg murkav*), directs the soul toward the textured landscape of lived experience. This latter state of pleasure derives from the superconscious connection that the soul makes with its own latent powers and capacities waiting to be cultivated through conscious life.

Unable to guide the soul toward the pleasures of self-actualization without the mediating force of will, pleasure remains a distant surrounding power (מַקִּיף הָרָחוֹק), irrational by nature and therefore removed from the realm of structured experience. Will, on the other hand, is the nearby surrounding power[2] (מַקִּיף הַקָּרוֹב), exerting a more direct influence upon consciousness by seeking to accommodate reason in the pursuit of its objectives.

Nonetheless, the origin of will in the soul, referred to as the **supreme will** (רָצוֹן עֶלְיוֹן, *ratzon elyon*, lit., "higher will"), is super-rational. Of this level is said in the Kabbalah, "there is no reason for [i.e., behind, motivating] will." Will is higher, that is, it precedes the origin of intellect in the unconscious of the soul (the level of *mocha stima'ah* to be explained later).

The force of will that concurs with the dictates of reason is concomitantly referred to as **common will** (רָצוֹן תַּחְתּוֹן, *ratzon tachton*, lit., "lower will").[3] Whereas the source of supreme will is hidden from view in the super-rational, common will is shaped by one's conscious and reason-guided deliberation. Therefore, it is situated below the origin of intellect in the soul.

pleasure	Simple	experience of one's source in Divinity
	structured	experience of one's latent capacities
will	supreme	super-rational will
	common	will that accords with reason

Intellect and Character-Attributes

The internal powers,[4] expressed through consciousness, can be grouped as well into two underlying branches of experience: the **intellect** (שֵׂכֶל, *sechel*) and **character-attributes** (מִדּוֹת, *midot*).

The intellect is the repository wherein lie one's higher powers of consciousness, those associated with the functions of intelligence. The realm of the character-attributes, on the other hand, is the territory of one's emotion and instinct. These are the conscious properties of the soul which can be disciplined by intellect but which nevertheless possess a reason all their own.

The conscious realm of intellect is ultimately grounded within the superconscious through a force referred to as the **hidden intellect** (שֵׂכֶל נֶעְלָם, *sechel ne'elam*). This hidden root of intelligence is responsible for generating the **revealed intellect** (שֵׂכֶל גָּלוּי, *sechel galui*) that manifests itself through normal cognition and thought. Together, the hidden and revealed intellects are the two basic modes of intellect-based experience.

The type of experience associated with the character-attributes possesses a dual character as well. Those specific attributes of our character which are generated through emotive experience are referred to as the **aroused** (מֻרְגָּשׁ, *murgash*) branch of the character-attributes, while those properties which express themselves through instinctive behavior are called the **innate** (מֻטְבָּע, *mutba*) branch of the character-attributes.

Intellect	hidden	hidden root of intelligence
	revealed	conscious intellect
character attributes	aroused	aroused emotion
	innate	instinctive behavior

Aside from these four branches of experience— pleasure, will, intellect, and character-attributes— there exist three vehicles of self-expression, the garments, which enable these powers to achieve concrete form. Each identified property of the soul requires a unique mode of expression suited to its particular character and function. The three garments of the soul are **thought** (מַחֲשָׁבָה, *machshavah*), **speech** (דִּבּוּר, *dibbur*), and **action** (מַעֲשֶׂה, *ma'aseh*). As the idiom "garments" implies, they enclothe the powers, providing them with the means to shape meaningful experience and behavior.

The first two of the soul's garments—thought and speech—manifest a dual nature. Each one of them subdivides into two aspects or dimensions. Action, on the other hand, retains a single and unified expressive character.

Let us now explore each of these in greater detail so that we may complete our survey of the thirteen experiential modes characterizing the inner life.

Thought

There are two distinct levels of thought: **focused thought** (עִיּוּן, *iyun*) and **random reflection** (הִרְהוּר, *hirhur*). Focused thought is the capacity for concentrated and penetrating analysis, leading to profound conceptual abstraction. This form of thought, also known as **intelligent thought** (מַחֲשֶׁבֶת שֵׂכֶל, *machshevet sechel*), starts out by "enclothing" one's concrete intellect and then proceeds to engage higher levels of intellect, to the point of activating the superconscious root of intelligence from whose infinite depth all true insight is born.

Random reflection, on the other hand, is the kind of free-flowing and non-critical thought which, though lacking in focus and depth, is rich in associative imagery. If left totally untempered, this **perpetual drift of thought** (מַחֲשָׁבָה מְשׁוֹטֶטֶת תָּמִיד, *machshavah m'shotetet tamid*) can cause one's cognitive powers to totally diffuse, leaving the soul feeling lost and wasted. When harnessed, however, in the service of meaningful contemplation, it can enable one to discover new horizons of thought that he may have never encountered through the discipline of focused thought alone.

Although the medium of thought can serve as a vehicle for developing either one's depth or range of cognitive experience, its ultimate purpose remains the achievement of self-enlightenment. The garment of speech, on the other hand, is primarily employed in the service of enlightening others. Here too we will encounter two distinct modes of expression that endow speech with a dual character and purpose.

Speech

While speech manifests itself through two differing modes, **profound speech** (דִּבּוּר פְּנִימִי, *dibbur penimi*) and **superficial speech** (דִּבּוּר חִצוֹנִי, *dibbur chitzoni*), its objective remains a unified one: the sharing of one's thoughts and feelings with others.

These two fundamental styles of communication involve, respectively, "words spoken from the heart" (דְּבָרִים הַיּוֹצְאִים מִן הַלֵּב, *devarim hayotzim min halev*) or "words that issue only from the lips and outward" (מִן הַשָּׂפָה וְלַחוּץ, *min hasafah velachutz*).

One can properly appreciate the difference between these two modes of speech by pondering two instances where God transmitted His own words into reality. The first of these instances was the occasion of Creation itself, when God issued ten utterances out of which the entirety of Creation emerged. Our sages teach us that these utterances are, as it were, "words of a layman" or "common speech" (מִילִין דְּהֶדְיוֹטָא, *milin dehedyota*). This implies that the act of Creation did not elicit the quality or depth of Divine communication that we find in the second instance of God's speech, the revelation at Sinai.

The Ten Commandments spoken at Sinai and engraved upon the tablets of the covenant can be figuratively described as "words spoken from the heart" of God. The first of the Ten Commandments— "I am the GOD your God"—begins with the Hebrew word אָנֹכִי, interpreted by our sages as an acronym for the words אֲנָא נַפְשִׁי כְּתָבִית יְהָבִית ("I have written and conveyed My very Essence," *ana nafshi ketavit yehavit*).[5] At Sinai, God projected Himself into the world with a revelatory force that challenged even the display of Divine power that accompanied Creation.

In truth, all speech is an attempt to project oneself into reality. Just as the extent to which one's voice projects depends upon the depth from which it originates, so too the identity conveyed by one's voice manifests itself differently depending on whether one speaks from the heart or merely from the lips.[6] Insofar as the deeper significance behind Creation remained camouflaged until Sinai, the ten supreme utterances that brought the universe into being were merely a kind of Divine "lip service." Without the disclosure at Sinai of God's program for Creation, man's existence would have remained superficial and barren of genuine meaning.

The reason for this discrepancy in Divine communication can be identified as the need God saw for adequately preparing the world to receive the import of His Torah. Our sages teach us that "words spoken from the heart penetrate the heart." Without a heart properly prepared for penetration, the conveyance of Divine essence through the revelation of the Torah at the time of Creation would have been in vain. From that first moment up to the arrival of Israel at Sinai, God set about fashioning the heart of a people that would warrant revealing Himself in all His profound glory to mankind.

Creation thus represents the process whereby God began preparing the heart of man to properly absorb the Divine knowledge and light contained in the Torah. The sixth and final day of Creation—when the physical heart of man was formed—hints, according to our sages,[7] at the sixth day of the Jewish month of *Sivan*, the day on which the Torah was given and thus the day upon which the world's entire survival was predicated. The sixth day of the week remains for all time the day upon which we prepare for the holiness of the Sabbath, upon which the Torah was also originally given.[8]

Just as the "earthly" speech that brought Creation into being was ultimately aimed at preparing the world for its future perfection, so too should man seek to make his mundane, daily discourse enhance his receptivity to wisdom and light. This is best demonstrated by the example of the classic Torah scholar. Primarily interested in sharing profound words of Torah, he rarely addresses temporal issues. Yet when he does, his "mundane talk" begs inspection,[9] because it reflects the manner in which he understands the created realm, which his heartfelt words of Torah aim to rectify.[10]

profound speech	words spoken from the heart	Ten Commandments at Sinai
superficial speech	words spoken from the lips	ten utterances of Creation

Action

As indicated above, action does not branch into derivative modes, as is the case with thought and speech. The essence of physical action is the pursuit of a direct and unmediated involvement with the outside world. Regardless of how that involvement is executed, deeply or superficially, the essential act remains the same. Such distinctions as are normally attached to our actions, such as good or evil, derive from an external value-frame that exists independent of the action itself. The action remains nothing more than a mute demonstration of Creation interacting with itself.[11]

Although action is the ultimate in "anonymous" self-expression, intrinsically void of the personal meaning that one attaches to it, it nevertheless paradoxically allows one to leave a unique mark upon Creation. For whereas the garments of thought and speech are inseparably identified with the soul that produces them, they nevertheless disappear from reality unless immortalized through some objective action, such as writing. Consequently, it can be said that action aspires toward the same goal as speech — the projection of self into reality — but within a context of anonymity that assures one's effect upon the world a measure of permanence and autonomy.[12]

The ultimate vehicle for constructive self-expression is the act of performing a *mitzvah*. The democratic nature of action, equally accessible to all regardless of stature, makes *mitzvah*-performance the great equalizer of Jewish experience and the ideal platform for demonstrating the unity of Israel. Possessing great intelligence or spiritual depth does not qualify a particular individual's *mitzvah* as any more real or significant than that of another with lesser qualities. By engaging all Jews in a common physical dialogue with Creation, *mitzvah*-performance allows one to serve as a vehicle for expressing the perfectly uniform Divine essence that renders the tiny and the great within Creation virtually indistinct.[13]

The quintessential *mitzvah*, according to Jewish tradition, is that of philanthropy (צְדָקָה, *tzedakah*). As such, it specifically engages the property of anonymity associated with action as a whole. The highest level of *tzedakah*-giving is said to be that where neither the giver nor the receiver are aware of each other's identity. The act of *tzedakah*, as derived from the root *tzedek* (צֶדֶק, "justice"), promotes the just redistribution of nature's bounty—a gift of God—amongst all His creatures who equally deserve its benefit.

In general, it can be said that at each level of self-expression, from thought to action, the soul proceeds toward a greater degree of involvement with external reality. This is even reflected in the language that we employ when relating thought, speech, and deed to the world around us.[14] We say that we think *about* something, as if detachedly considering it from all angles equally. However, when it comes to speech, we say that we talk *to* or *with* someone, implying a specific directionality in our relationship to the person though still separate from him. Finally, in regard to actions, we say that we act *upon* something—all distance being eliminated as subject and object actually touch. An even more intimate state of merger is hinted at by the idiom "to do something," which, lacking a preposition altogether, suggests a total identification between the doer and the deed.

Notes:

1. There are of course exceptions to this rule, as in the case to be discussed later of one who exhibits a capacity for self-sacrifice. Here, the more sublime force of *emunah* ("faith") eclipses the *oneg-* ("pleasure"-) imperative and impels one's will to overrule it.

2. In terms of the five dimensions of soul cited at the beginning of our discussion, the distant *makif* is identified with *yechidah* while the nearby *makif* corresponds to *chayah*.

3. See *Likueti Torah, Shir Hashirim* 47d-48a.

4. For all that follows, see also *What You Need to Know About Kabbalah*, chapters 6 and 7.

5. This commandment, along with its companion, the prohibition against worshipping other gods, was communicated directly from the "mouth of Divine Might." As the only commandments containing the first-person pronoun *Anochi* ("I"), they express God's will to address man directly from His essence. The account of Creation, on the other hand, is formulated entirely in the objective third-person.

6. Rectified speech, emanating from the heart, is termed in Kabbalah the unification between Jacob, who represents the raw power of *kol*—"voice" ("the voice is the voice of Jacob"), and Rachel, who symbolizes the power to transform *kol* into *dibur*, "speech."

7. See *Rashi* to Genesis 1:31.

8. This fact itself indicates that Torah-speech is of another kind than daily speech, inasmuch as God uttered no speech-of-Creation on Shabbat. See *Tanya, Kuntres Acharon* 9. This is also one reason why, in the recitation of the Shabbat-night *kiddush*, the words יום הששי are joined to the following paragraph, which describes Shabbat.

9. *Avodah Zarah* 19b.

10. In a similar vein, the Talmud (*Pesachim* 117a) recounts how a particular sage would always begin his discourse with a few "words of jest," indicating that the heart's responsiveness to words of humor enhances its receptiveness to the words of wisdom to follow.

11. For this reason, the performance of an action alone does not always provide sufficient criteria for establishing the degree of merit or liability that can be attached to it. The merit of an action is most often determined by the intention behind it. The intention derives from the autonomous realm of thought. A minimal degree of conscious intention is necessary in order to define an act as either a *mitzvah* or a transgression. Even more remarkably, a particular intention can actually transform an act normally assumed to be a *mitzvah* into the opposite—as well as vice versa. Thus we see that a simple physical action cannot be intrinsically defined as possessing one value or another.

12. The differing degrees of expressiveness associated with these three garments can best be viewed in terms of the role that "letters" (signifying classes of media) play at each level of "enclothement." For a complete discussion of this topic, see *Tanya, Igeret HaKodesh*, chapter 19. Another way to envision their relationship is by meditating on the form of the letter *hei*: ה. The horizontal and vertical lines that touch (together they form a letter *dalet*) correspond to the garments of thought (the expansive roof of the letter) and speech (the right line extending downward). The detached *yud*

at the bottom left represents the autonomous garment of action.

13. See *Tanya*, chapter 46 for a discussion of how the holiness that is "uniform for every soul" of Israel expresses itself through the performance of *mitzvot*.

14. The following phenomena exist in the Hebrew language, as well.

5

A Summary
of the Thirteen
Measures-of-Experience
in the Soul

the root of the soul	**powers**	**transcendent**	pleasure	simple	faith (the simple song) (א)
				composite	delight of intellect (the 2-part song) (ב)
					delight of the emotions (the 3-part song) (ג)
					delight of the speech (the 4-part song) (ד)
			will	supreme	beyond reason and understanding (ה)
				common	in accordance with reason and understanding (ו)
		immanent	intellect	hidden	koa'ch hamaskil (ז)
				revealed	chochmah (bitul) (ח) binah (simchah) (ט)
					da'at (yichud) (י)
			character attributes	arroused	chesed (ahavah) (כ) gevurah (yirah) (ל)
					tiferet (rachamim) (מ)
				innate	netzach (bitachon) (נ) hod (temimut) (ס)
					yesod (emet) (ע)
					malchut (shiflut) (פ)
	garments		thought	focused thought	intelligent thought (צ)
				random reflection	perpetual drift of thought (ק)
			speech	profound	words spoken from the heart (ר)
				superficial	words that issue only from the lips outward (ש)
			action		equalizing great and small (ת)

A Summary of the Thirteen Measures-of-Experience in the Soul 5

Having completed our survey of the garments, we arrive at thirteen measures of experience comprised of six pairs—corresponding to the branches of pleasure, will, intellect, character-attributes, thought, and speech—and the single measure associated with the branch of action.

Each of the six pairs can be thought of as defining a particular scale for assessing reality. These scales, each built upon a unique conceptual distinction, can be summarized as follows:

1. In the realm of pleasure: the difference between simple and composite—a measure of structure.

2. In the realm of will: the difference between supreme and common—a measure of dominance.

3. In the realm of intellect: the difference between hidden and revealed—a measure of consciousness.

4. In the realm of character-attributes: the difference between aroused and instinctive—a measure of affectation.

5. In the realm of thought: the difference between focus and range—a measure of object-orientation.

6. In the realm of speech: the difference between interior and exterior—a measure of self-projection.

These six independent sets of coordinates are the immediate conceptual base upon which the varied range of spiritual experience is founded. Each of these scales alone could be employed to explain any number of phenomena in life. When a particular distinction is adopted in consciousness, it simply means that one is asserting the specific realm of the soul identified with that conceptual measure.

However, any of these distinctions could also be used to explain phenomena that lie outside the realm formally associated with it. For example, the application of the dominance-scale to a property of the intellect, such as *da'at*,[1] indicates that one is viewing that property from the perspective of will, i.e., as to whether it supersedes common intellect or is subservient to it. Likewise, relating to emotion in terms of interior or exterior (the scale identified above with the property of speech)[2] indicates that one is assessing emotion in light of the expressive qualities associated with speech—that is, in terms of the extent to which it possesses projective potency.[3]

Applying these scales freely and flexibly to all levels of one's experience allows for an infinite variety of perspective and interpretation when it comes to conducting the encounter between the self and the external reality.

Notes:

1. As in the usage of the terms higher *da'at* (דעת עליון) and lower *da'at* (דעת תחתון).

2. As in the distinction made between inner (emotive) excitation (התפעלות פנימית) and superficial (emotive) excitation (התפעלות חצונית).

3. The more internal an emotion's source, the more potency it possesses, potency that allows for its projection into another soul. This lends deeper meaning to the statement of our sages (*cf. Berachot* 6b): דברים היוצאים מן הלב נכנסים אל הלב, "words that issue from the heart [—and not just the lips] will enter into the heart [of another]." See above, p. 64.

6

The Splendor
of the Soul

Twenty-Two Flowering Offshoots
of the Powers and Garments

the root of the soul

powers — transcendent	pleasure	simple	faith (the simple song) (א)	
		composite	delight of intellect (the 2-part song) (ב)	
			delight of the emotions (the 3-part song) (ג)	
			delight of the speech (the 4-part song) (ד)	
	will	supreme	beyond reason and understanding (ה)	
		common	in accordance with reason and understanding (ו)	
powers — immanent	intellect	hidden	koa'ch hamaskil (ז)	
		revealed	chochmah (bitul) (ח)	binah (simchah) (ט)
			da'at (yichud) (י)	
	character attributes	arroused	chesed (ahavah) (כ)	gevurah (virah) (ל)
			tiferet (rachamim) (מ)	
		innate	netzach (bitachon) (נ)	hod (temimut) (ס)
			yesod (emet) (ע)	
			malchut (shiflut) (פ)	
garments	thought	focused thought	intelligent thought (צ)	
		random reflection	perpetual drift of thought (ק)	
	speech	profound	words spoken from the heart (ר)	
		superficial	words that issue only from the lips outward (ש)	
	action		equalizing great and small (ת)	

The Splendor of the Soul 6
Twenty-Two Flowering Offshoots
of the Powers and Garments

Having completed our consideration of the general categories of human experience, we may now proceed to identify and discuss the express properties and functions of the soul which comprise our experience in particular. It is from these intrinsic elements that we extract our parallel vision of the Divine subjectivity behind Creation.

Kabbalah teaches us that at every level of created being—from the perfected realm of *Atzilut* (Divine Emanation) to the deficient plane of our own earthly existence—there exist ten *sefirot* (סְפִירוֹת, Divine emanations) around which that reality is constructed. Each of these *sefirot* is given a name describing its unique role in the fashioning of reality. At every level, the *sefirot* continue to assert themselves beyond their initial manifestation in the process of creation, enduring as the genetic structure of all experience. Here, we shall refer to them in terms of the role they play in the metaphysical evolution of created being, especially as they operate in the world of *Atzilut*, the model of perfected reality against which all subsequent realms of Creation are measured.

Each of the *sefirot* possesses both an external as well as an internal dimension. The external dimension of each *sefirah* is identified with the functional role that it plays in the process of Creation; its internal dimension is identified with the hidden motivational force, which inspires its activity. Even more so than with respect to the external dimension of the *sefirot*, their inner dimension can only be appreciated in context of how it manifests itself in the Jewish soul. Given the Divine derivation of our soul, we can understand how an analysis of its essential properties and powers can serve as the best vehicle for achieving insight into God's own inscrutable being.

Chasidut describes the inspirational force behind each *sefirah*. While the Kabbalistic names of the *sefirot* serve well to express the Divine effect that each of these powers has upon Creation, only the terms put forth by *Chasidut* reveal the inner dimension of each *sefirah*.[1]

As we now begin to explore the ways in which the *sefirot* manifest themselves in the soul, we will identify them by both the generic Kabbalistic designation as well as by the expression or term used in *Chasidut* to describe their inner aspect. The two frames of reference will combine to give us a fuller appreciation of how the soul mirrors the Divine face of Creation.

Altogether, there are twenty-two branches at this outermost level of the tree. Of these, seventeen derive from the powers and five from the garments. The five branches of the garments are direct extensions of those described at the previous level and consequently will not be reviewed again. Of the seventeen offshoots associated with the powers, six are related to the superconscious realm while eleven exist within consciousness.[2]

These eleven, corresponding to the intellect and character-attributes, represent a variety of intellectual and emotive functions through which it is possible to achieve insight into the complete spectrum of Divine expression within Creation. The cognitive forces of one's intellect correspond to the Divine powers of *chochmah* ("wisdom"), *binah* ("understanding"), and *da'at* ("knowledge"). The various character-attributes correspond to the emotive powers of *chesed* ("loving-kindness"), *gevurah* ("might"), and *tiferet* ("beauty"), and the instinctive powers of *netzach* ("victory"), *hod* ("acknowledgment"), *yesod* ("foundation"), and *malchut* ("kingdom").

The six superconscious properties of the soul correspond to the hidden *sefirah* of *keter* ("crown"). We will begin our final exploration of the soul, and through it of Divine reality, at this supreme point of origin in Creation.

The Realm of Keter

Keter

The *sefirah* of *keter* (כֶּתֶר, "crown") is the source of all superconscious experience. The image of the crown evokes a sense of the sublime Divine energy that hovers just above Creation—beyond reason and understanding—encompassing the universe while eluding its awareness at the same time.

Keter is divided into two major substrates referred to in Kabbalah as *Atik Yomin* (עַתִּיק יוֹמִין, "the Ancient of Days") and *Arich Anpin* (אֲרִיךְ אַנְפִּין, "the Elongated Countenance"). In the terminology of *Chasidut*, these two manifestations of *keter* are synonymous with the superconscious powers of pleasure and will.

Pleasure, as we saw above, divides into two derivative states: simple and composite. These two states in turn translate into two identified properties of superconscious experience:

1. **faith** (אֱמוּנָה, *emunah*)—the totally unstructured superconscious state whereby the soul remains completely submerged within its Divine root-of-origin.

2. **pleasure** (תַּעֲנוּג, *ta'anug*)—the composite state of
   pleasure that overtakes the soul as it experiences
   the texture of its own innate capacities and
   powers. This pleasure, as we will see, takes three
   forms—corresponding to three categories of
   conscious power latent within the soul.

The lowest stratum of *keter*, the state of
superconscious will, itself possesses a higher and a
lower aspect; thus, we arrive at a total of six offshoots
springing from the three heads of keter: the single
manifestation of faith, three of pleasure, and two of
will.

Let us now briefly expound upon each of these
superconscious properties, which comprise the full
spectrum of surrounding powers in one's soul.

Faith

The supreme head of *keter*—faith—resides at the
hidden juncture where the soul clings to its source in
Divine essence (*atzmut*). It is this rooting within God's
essence that endows the soul with eternal life, as
suggested by the verse: "You who cling to GOD, your
God, are alive all of you this day,"[3] alluding to the
unending day of eternity.

The state of pleasure associated with faith is
completely simple, meaning that it is entirely abstract

and unstructured, void of even superconscious sensation. It refers to a state which is not as much pleasure as the *anticipation* of pleasure—that ultimate pleasure that will derive in days to come from the revelation within Creation of the Divine essence, demonstrating the absolute origin of all things within Divinity.

Consequently, the superconscious state of faith in the soul gives rise to both a deeply ingrained belief in one's origins as well as a concomitant faith in the destiny of Creation. The mutual embrace of both these parameters endows all the subsequent powers of one's soul with the foundation of belief in the underlying unity of existence, in spite of the apparently unavoidable antagonism and conflict that marks the encounter between the infinite and the finite.

Having its root in the inscrutable realm of the Divine essence, the essential state of faith is one that cannot be apprehended through logic or reason. Nevertheless, various characteristics of the Jewish soul—such as its capacity to sustain the paradoxes of existence or its willingness to sacrifice life for the sake of faith—point to its super-rational influence and force. The capacity to transcend the limitations of one's mind and body derives from the soul's connection through faith to the Divine essence that generates the ultimate paradox of Creation: the emergence of finite reality from God's infinite Being.

Pleasure

The intermediate head of *keter*—pleasure—is the base of an entirely different kind of superconscious pleasure, the hidden pleasure which derives from the anticipation of one's innate capacities-of-self being engaged through conscious experience in uncovering the Divinity within Creation.[4] Pleasure implies the soul's coming-to-terms with its Divine mandate, acknowledging external reality as the framework within which it is meant to cultivate its full potential, and savoring the specific powers endowed it by God in service of that end.

As a superconscious frame of reference in the soul, pleasure represents the root of one's subjective assessment of the world. It is here where the intrinsic values that the soul employs in measuring experience have their ultimate origin. It is also from here that the innate aesthetic sense that informs one's ongoing probe of external reality derives.

The axiomatic values super-consciously uncovered through pleasure are consciously applied through the many immanent powers that have their ultimate root in this hidden realm of *keter*. As these powers are willed into consciousness, pleasure enclothes itself within them to produce three distinct varieties of superconscious pleasure:

1. The pleasure experienced through one's intellectual function,

2. The pleasure experienced through emotive experience, and

3. The pleasure experienced through speech—a paradigm for all the various powers of self-expression.[5]

This latter variety of pleasure should be thought of as that which is achieved through the act of cathartic release. The constructive discharge of creative tension accumulated within the soul brings with it a superconscious sensation of climax and resolution. Speech and the sexual act are the most potent examples of activity generating this kind of sensation—and as such are often equated in Kabbalah as possessing similar potential for both creative use and abuse.

Will

The third and final head of *keter*—will—is, as we discussed earlier, initially inspired by the state of pleasure. As the force that propels one into consciousness and then directs him toward pleasurable experience, will is the power motivating one to seek gratifying outlets for his intellect and character attributes.

Although its immediate direction comes from the superconscious realm of pleasure, the executive force of will is actually more intimately allied in *keter* with the head of faith, from where it inherits the capacity to actually suspend gratification when faith so dictates. As opposed to pleasure, which, when void of its own inner sense of faith, may mobilize will in the pursuit of transient pleasure, faith harnesses one's will in the service of more lasting objectives. This often results in the power of will being employed to resist action rather than initiate it, should such action be deemed as jeopardizing one's essential call of faith.

Both these manifestations of will are identified with the superconscious quality referred to above as supreme will, which is thoroughly inscrutable, totally beyond reason and understanding. Supreme will expresses itself through one's determination to experience the essential vitality of his soul, yet in accordance with the dictates of faith—both constituting Divine mandates to which the soul is sworn.

More closely aligned with the realm of intellect is the common will,[6] which, while also originating in *keter*, nevertheless accords with a rational design for living. This form of will also seeks to promote the objectives of *keter*, yet only through coordination with one's reason. For instance, the will to live is, as we mentioned, a prime example of supreme will. However, if an individual falls ill, it will be he his common-will that will impel him to do everything in his power to seek reliable and efficient medical care. The untempered force of supreme will acting by itself in such a situation might bring one to act impulsively and without discretion, jeopardizing his ultimate aim.

The less successful one is in achieving reasonable objectives in life, the more likely it is that his supreme will is asserting itself too strongly. The ability of common will to override the irrational tendencies of one's higher will paradoxically derives as well from its connection to faith. In particular, it expresses one's faith in the rectified intellect of Torah, which serves as the instrument of Divine purpose in the world.

The Realm of the Intellect

There are four properties represented in the realm of the intellect. The first — the *ko'ach hamaskil* — serves as a bridge between *keter* and revealed intellect. It is synonymous with the branch of the soul identified earlier as the hidden intellect. The remaining three properties of the intellect — *chochmah*, *binah*, and *da'at* — all represent revealed powers of intelligence, offshoots of one's conscious intellect. Each of these powers makes its own unique contribution to the awareness that takes root in consciousness.

Ko'ach Hamaskil and Chochmah

Chochmah (חָכְמָה, "wisdom") is the male-principle at work in one's intellect. It is the innovative and essentially unpredictable force that produces those spontaneous insights which we nurture to maturity through the companion power of *binah*, the female principle of intelligence.

The inner essence of *chochmah* is **bitul** (בְּטוּל, "self-nullification"). In Kabbalah, the Hebrew word *chochmah* is often explained as a transposition of the two words כֹּחַ מָה, "the power of *mah*"—*mah* being a code-word for *bitul* (as seen from the verse whereby Moses nullifies himself before Israel: "What [מָה] are we [Aaron and I] that you murmur against us!"[7] The essence of *bitul* consists of negating one's self in context of affirming the Divine source to which one is ultimately connected. As a result of *bitul*, one's individual existence is no longer experienced as an independent and self-sustaining fixture of Creation. By grafting one's consciousness to the ground of all being, one's mind becomes a conduit for Divine wisdom, which expresses itself through flashes of spontaneous intuitive insight. As bolts of lightning, these flashes of insight may lack gravity and permanence, but nevertheless serve to spark one's subsequent pursuit of meaningful knowledge.

These flashes ultimately derive from a hidden source within *keter* referred to in *Chasidut* as **ko'ach hamaskil** (כֹּחַ הַמַּשְׂכִּיל, "the enlightening power") or in Kabbalah as "the hidden brain" (מוֹחָא סְתִימָאָה, *mocha stima'ah*).[8] *Ko'ach hamaskil* represents both the sum of one's cognitive potential and the power that brings it to light. As reflected in *chochmah* itself, the enlightening brain enables one to identify the core abstraction or nothingness (אַיִן, *ayin*) that underlies all true knowledge of reality.[9]

The image of the lightning bolt, which is often employed as a symbol of the spontaneous insight revealed in *chochmah*, once again points to the force of *chashmal* resident within one's soul. As we saw earlier, *chashmal* is the radiant energy that results from the soul's oscillation between states of concealment and revelation. The bolts of insight that emerge from the darkness beyond consciousness can be viewed as the product of a similar dynamic exchange between the hidden enlightening power—the force of *chash*—and the revealed intellect (שֵׂכֶל גָּלוּי, *sechel galui*) of *chochmah*—the force of *mal*.[10]

chash	ko'ach hamaskil
mal (1)	contracting channels
mal (2)	conscious *chochmah*

Binah

Binah (בִּינָה, "understanding") is the cognitive force that absorbs the nuclear seed of *chochmah* and articulates it into fine detail through a process of associative analysis referred to as "understanding one thing out of another."[11] This process of understanding entails more than just deductively extracting a model of reality from the "genetic" shorthand of *chochmah*; it also involves the ability to intuit a more inclusive reality than that encoded within *chochmah* itself.

Once having attained the mature understanding of *binah*, the soul swells with delight at its achievement. The inner essence of *binah* is thus identified in *Chasidut* as **simchah** (שִׂמְחָה, "joy"). *Simchah* is the essential response of one's soul to felt accomplishment. The very word in Hebrew for "accomplishment" (הַשָּׂגָה) is generally associated with intellectual achievement, particularly the kind represented by *binah*'s elaboration of *chochmah* into full-bodied constructions of thought.

The male and female *sefirot* of *chochmah* and *binah* are depicted in the *Zohar* as "two inseparable companions." Every thought we experience is predicated upon the collaboration between these two cognitive principles. When we find each of them expressed in Kabbalah as an autonomous conceptual structure (a פַּרְצוּף, *partzuf*), they are referred to as *Abba*

(אַבָּא, "father") and *Ima* (אִמָּא, "mother"). Their sustained interaction is the precondition for the subsequent birth in one's soul of the character attributes, appropriately called the "children" in Kabbalah.

The most common Scriptural expression applied to the *sefirah* of *binah* is Psalms 113:9: "the mother of children does rejoice." The identification of *binah* with the mother follows from an hermeneutic interpretation of Proverbs 2:3: "'If you call out for understanding'—do not read 'if' (אִם) but rather 'mother' (אֵם)," implying that the verse read "and you shall call *binah* 'mother.'"

Three distinct stages of *simchah* can be identified in the advance toward motherhood, each of which corresponds to a state of emerging *binah*. The first is the *simchah* of the very anticipation of conceiving a child. This expression of faith in one's maternal destiny[12] provides woman with the power to absorb the male essence from which new life will form. It is reflected in *binah* as the joy one experiences in embracing the raw insight of *chochmah* out of which one hopes to produce mature thought.

The second stage of *simchah* which characterizes *binah* is that associated with the now-pregnant woman anticipating the moment of birth. This *simchah*, which extends throughout pregnancy and facilitates the healthy development of embryonic life,[13] parallels the delight associated with *binah*'s vigorously elaborating a new idea.

Finally, the *simchah* that overtakes every mother at the decisive moment of birth, when all doubt and fear is resolved in her soul, is mirrored by the definitive joy of *binah* in producing a mature thought or idea — a joy whose effect is felt through a range of affective responses triggered in one's being.

Da'at

The *sefirah* of **da'at** (דַּעַת, "knowledge"), the final Divine power to manifest itself through the intellect, is unusual insofar as in general it is only counted as one of the ten *sefirot* when *keter* is not considered.[14] This is because *keter* and *da'at* represent two alternative expressions of a single Divine force: that which enables the soul to sustain diametrically opposed states of being at one and the same time.[15]

While still enclothed within *keter* this force expresses itself as the superconscious power to endure the fundamental paradoxes of existence. When caused to descend into consciousness and *da'at*, it manifests as the capacity to both bind together (or unify) the conscious powers of *chochmah* and *binah* as well as bridge the opposing domains of the intellect and the emotive character attributes in the soul.[16]

Indeed, the term used to describe the inner essence of *da'at* in the soul is **yichud** (יְחוּד, "unification"). As opposed to being another stage in the elaboration of intellect, *da'at* signifies the power to unify and bridge, in the mind as well as in the heart, the conception of truth that one has already technically achieved through *chochmah* and *binah*. As a conscious expression of the power in *keter* to encompass all sides of reality, *da'at* seeks to erase the intrinsic boundaries that separate the knower from the known; but unlike *keter*, which abstracts reality, *da'at* pursues *yichud* through intense concentration upon that reality's identified form—whether it is physical or symbolic, concrete or abstract. It is this power to penetrate and attach oneself to reality, the basis of memory as well, that enables one to convert understanding into a force that vitalizes and inspires the character attributes as well as achieves expression through action and deed.

The strongest Scriptural indication of *da'at*'s unifying character can be found in the verse: "And Adam knew his wife Eve."[17] The verb "knew" is euphemistically used in this verse to denote the physical union of husband and wife. Its association with this most intimate form of *yichud* qualifies *da'at* in particular as a symbol of the merger between *chochmah* and *binah*, the male and female powers of one's intellect. Their unification is what facilitates the free and uninterrupted flow of new insight into the cognitive realm while at the same time allowing that insight to constantly mature and develop.[18]

What follows the unity attained in the intellect is a bond that *da'at* forges between the intellect and the emotions. Unfortunately, this latter bond does not exhibit the same intrinsic lasting character as the former. This is because the intellect and character attributes, though mutually affecting each other, are essentially autonomous domains. When indeed synchronized, *da'at* succeeds in opening up the character attributes to the enlightening power of one's intellect, thereby resolving much of the innate conflict that exists between the emotive attributes themselves.[19]

Because the emotions are essentially rooted in the superconscious realm,[20] it often happens that the character attributes elude *da'at* altogether, drawing their inspiration directly from *keter*. When asserted in this super-rational vein, the emotive attributes are said to express one's primal nature (טֶבַע רִאשׁוֹן, *teva rishon*). Man's ability to cultivate a more disciplined second nature (טֶבַע שֵׁנִי, *teva sheini*) is dependent upon the success of *da'at* in submitting raw emotion to the conclusions of reasoned (softened) analysis so that it may be refined and rectified. Once *da'at* leaves its mark on a particular character attribute, that property can then be aroused naturally without fearing any negative effect.[21]

Should the intellect and character attributes resist the mediation of *da'at* and persist in operating independently of each other,[22] the soul will be plagued by inner conflict. The direct consequence of this situation is the spiritual poverty that it brings to both one's intellectual and emotional life. Only when the channel of *da'at* serving as the line of communication between these two realms is completely open and active can one experience the synergy of an integrated and *yichud*-inspired spiritual life.

Just as *chochmah* and *binah* — which *da'at* unifies in the intellectual realm — are likened to a male and female, so here, the intellectual and emotive realms are relatively masculine and feminine. There is a difference though in the capacity that *da'at* plays in each case. The unification of the masculine and feminine aspects corresponding to *chochmah* and *binah* is based on the similarities between these two intellectual powers. But, the unification of mind and heart is based on uniting dissimilars, as the mind and the heart are opposite in nature.

In the terminology of the Bible, the first type of unification is described as "finding favor in one's eyes,"[23] while the second is described as "bearing favor in one's eyes."[24] Both types of unification are important and both are necessary and ultimately interdependent in our service of God.[25]

The Realm of the Character attributes

The full complement of character attributes in one's soul consists of both the emotive responses of his heart and the instinctive character-features manifest through his outer demeanor. The underlying branches of experience associated with these two sets of attributes were described above as the consciously aroused (*murgash*) *midot* and the innate (*mutba*) *midot*.[26]

The aroused properties of *chesed, gevurah,* and *tiferet* (corresponding in Kabbalistic anatomy to the two hands and the torso[27]) assert themselves ahead of the innate properties of *netzach, hod, yesod,* and *malchut* (which are associated with the lower limbs of the body) indicating that the emotions play an important role in inspiring one to act in line with his innate Godly features. This implies that while it is proper to consciously arouse oneself to action through the emotions, one's actual behavior should express itself as spontaneous, natural and stable, free of the conflict or compulsion that so often characterizes emotive experience.

In considering the transition from the intellect to the character attributes, it is important to once again emphasize that the force of *da'at* remains active within the realm of emotion and instinct,[28] and in fact, it enables the diverse properties within this realm to interact and harmonize. The process whereby one employs *da'at* to create greater consciousness and purposefulness within one's affective life, resulting in the differing emotions working together, is called *tikun hamidot* (תִּקּוּן הַמִּדּוֹת, "character rectification").

Chesed

Chesed (חֶסֶד, "loving-kindness"), the first of the seven character attributes in the soul, reflects the primary force that God employed in creating the world, as intimated in Psalms: "The world is constructed with *chesed.*"[29] The *sefirah* of *chesed* represents the underlying force of expansiveness and attraction that enabled the initial elements of Creation to propagate and flourish without losing their essential identification with one another.

Though tending toward diffusion, the force of *chesed* nevertheless impels Creation to emulate the all-embracing oneness of its Divine source—thereby redefining the expanding universe as one whose component elements are actually reaching out ultimately to unite with each other. This tendency becomes more and more evident as the universe approaches its final rectification.

The inner essence of *chesed*, its motivating force, is *ahavah* (אַהֲבָה, "love"). *Chesed* implies the capacity for attaching oneself to others freely and with unconditional love and benevolence.[30] Although each character attribute represents only one aspect of man's full affective potential, *chesed* is unique insofar as it can be discerned in all the subsequent character attributes as the force that impels them toward greatness. Referred to as the force of *gedulah* (גְּדֻלָּה, "largesse"),[31] *chesed* nurtures the other properties of one's soul into full maturity, thereby promoting the total development of character.[32]

Our father Abraham is identified in the Bible with *chesed*: "Give...*chesed* to Abraham"[33]; with *ahavah*, its inner essence: "the seed of Abraham, my loving one"[34]; and with its manifestation as *gedulah*: "the greatest man among the giants."[35]

Abraham's love, directed at all men equally, flowed out of the esteem with which he regarded the totality of God's Creation, of which man is the pinnacle. In every human being, Abraham saw a reflection of God's desire to unconditionally bestow goodness upon Creation, and this in turn inspired the same desire within him. Emulating his Creator, Abraham proceeded to provide physical and spiritual sustenance to all who passed his way, thereby nurturing humanity to greatness and reinstating the consciousness of God's abiding *chesed*.

Gevurah (Might)

The *sefirah* of *gevurah* (גְּבוּרָה, "might")—associated with the force of *din* (דִּין, severe Divine "judgment")—represents an opposing force in Creation to that of expansive *chesed*. The effect it has is to restrain the indiscriminate and unbridled inflation of the universe toward greater oneness. *Gevurah* seeks to preserve the intrinsic boundaries which God set for each and every element within Creation. In so doing, it promotes an increasing order and diversity within the expanding cosmos, disciplining the unifying force of *chesed* so as not to challenge or violate the individual integrity of any single element which God willed into autonomous being.

The inner essence of *gevurah* is **yirah** (יְרָאָה, "fear" or "awe").[36] *Yirah* represents the trepidation of the soul with regard to indiscriminately showering kindness upon others. Whereas *ahavah* impels one to give unconditionally, without concern for the other's worthiness to receive, *yirah* argues against doing so, out of concern that the precious store of human goodness not be squandered on one undeserving of its rewards. Consequently, every opportunity to bestow goodness upon others is assessed in terms of individual merit, so that one's giving is commensurate with the specific factors commending each situation.

On the other hand, *yirah* is just as influential in inspiring one to courageously uphold, even in the face of overwhelming opposition, another's right to the rewards which are justifiably due him. Should Divine justice dictate that someone be extended a particular benefit, the fear of heaven impels one to do all in his power to facilitate it. Concerned with maintaining proper measure and proportion within Creation, *gevurah* works to defend the boundaries of *din*, be they to one's advantage or disadvantage, requiring courage or trepidation.

Consequently, the antithetical position that *gevurah* often takes *vis-a-vis chesed* actually serves to promote the ultimate good of Creation. As complementary forces, the two actually work hand in hand—"the left arm [of *gevurah*] pushing away while the right arm [of *chesed*] brings near." *Gevurah* establishes the rigorous standard of merit that endows subsequent overtures of *chesed* with genuine value and meaning for the recipient.

Tiferet

Tiferet (תִּפְאֶרֶת, "beauty"), positioned along the "central axis" of the *sefirot*, is the Divine power within Creation that blends *chesed* and *gevurah*. *Tiferet* (from the root פאר) is one of the eight synonyms in Hebrew for "beauty,"[37] referring specifically to the kind that is associated with the harmonious blending of varying colors and forms.[38] Similarly, it is the power of *tiferet* which allows one to express a harmonious blend of the two spiritual poles of benevolence (*chesed*) and might (*gevurah*).

The inner essence that inspires *tiferet,* **rachamim** (רַחֲמִים, "compassion"), itself possesses two aspects. In its outer aspect, whereby it reflects the harmonizing character of *tiferet, rachamim* synthesizes the contrasting elements of *ahavah* and *yirah* into a force of discriminating compassion, directed at those whom one deems capable, if not worthy, of benefiting from one's goodness. This synthesis is achieved by employing reasoned advocacy (לִמּוּד זְכוּת, *leemud zechut*) in effecting an acceptable compromise between the counter-tendencies of *ahavah* and *yirah* that nonetheless favors *ahavah*. This reflects the principle stated in Kabbalah that *tiferet* always tends toward the right, the side of *chesed*.[39]

In its inner aspect, however, *rachamim* transcends the harmonic imperative, expressing itself instead as an autonomous power unrelated to the opposing forces of *ahavah* and *yirah* that precede it. In this aspect, *rachamim* is the raw empathic impulse compelling one to respond compassionately to the pain of others, oblivious to the reasoned arguments militating against such response. Descending directly from the super-rational *keter*, this inner spirit of *rachamim* impels one to pursue a higher imperative than either the altruism of *chesed* or the restraint of *gevurah*.

Netzach

The *sefirah* of **netzach** (נֶצַח, "victory") is the first of the four remaining *sefirot*—the instinctive character attributes within the soul which constitute one's constructive response to the enlightened need aroused in one's heart through the influence of intellect upon the emotions.

The word *netzach* implies many things: "victory" (נִצָחוֹן, *nitzachon*), "eternity" (נְצָחִיּוּת, *nitzchiut*), and "orchestration" (נִצּוּחַ, *nitzuach*). Common to all these ideas is a sense of the initiative and persistence necessary in order to overcome the inertial opposition preventing one from translating thought and feeling into positive action. "Victory" assumes initiative; "eternity" implies persistence; and "orchestration" presupposes a creative plan that employs both these qualities to its advantage.

The inner essence of *netzach* is **bitachon** (בִּטָחוֹן, "confidence"), the force that derives from the Divine promise[40] of assistance assured to all who strive to rectify the world. This Heavenly guarantee of success is conditional, however, upon one's acknowledging the Divine source of his power and might,[41] thus affirming his essential role as an instrument of God's purpose in Creation.

While infusing one with supreme self-confidence, the quality of *bitachon* at the same time impels one to mobilize his innate resources toward designing a realistic plan for achieving success. The inner counsel generated through *netzach* and its companion power, *hod*, accounts for their frequent association in Kabbalah with the counseling kidneys[42] referred by our sages as symbolic of instinctive moral wisdom. These powers of "wise assurance," as *netzach* and *hod* are also called, provide a basis for the consistent vision and resolve that serve as fundamental prerequisites for victory and success.

Hod

The *sefirah* of **hod** (הוֹד, "acknowledgment"), a companion power to the victory of *netzach*, expresses itself through two fundamentally-linked forces in Creation. The first, that of acknowledgment—as intimated by the root of *hod* appearing in the words for "praise" and "thanksgiving" (הוֹדָיָה, *hodayah*), "acknowledgment" (הוֹדָאָה, *hoda'ah*), and "confession" (וִדּוּי, *veedui*)—represents the capacity to acknowledge a supreme power or intelligence exerting authority over oneself.[43] The second force, which follows out of the first, is that of "glory" (*hod*, הוֹד). This resplendent aura of majesty is projected by that acknowledged higher power upon one who resigns himself in just such a spirit of acknowledgment.[44]

The inner essence of *hod* is **temimut** (תְּמִימוּת, "sincerity"), a combination of the innocence and earnestness that go into producing unshakable commitment to a chosen path. Whereas the *bitachon* of *netzach* enables one to thrust forward, forcefully overcoming all opposition to action, the *temimut* of *hod* provides a complementary anchor in the soul allowing one to steadfastly hold his proper course even as his active momentum, advancing toward creative fulfillment, threatens his balance and perspective.

Hod is the distanced posture of acknowledgment, which allows one to maintain a focused perspective regarding his Divine destiny, as hinted in the verse: "From afar God becomes apparent to me."[45] In this sense, the force of *hod* can be thought of as internal radar guiding one toward an unseen destination by amplifying the "echo" (הֵד, *hed*, from the same root as הוֹד) that it produces in the soul.

Together, the assertiveness of *bitachon* and the steadfastness of *temimut* help balance the soul as it proceeds toward realizing its fundamental objective in life—the edification of self and other through word and deed. In Kabbalistic imagery, the *sefirot* of *netzach* and *hod* correspond to the legs, stabilizing the body while propelling it forward. The left leg of *temimut* provides the steadying force that bolsters one against spiritual fatigue by fixing his consciousness on a distant yet radiant source of energy. The right leg of *bitachon* serves to advance the soul toward that source, enabling it to overcome the adversity in its path. The analogy to walking is particularly apt in view of the verse that states, "He who walks with simple sincerity [תֹּם] will walk confidently [בֶּטַח]."[46]

Yesod

The *sefirah* of **yesod** (יְסוֹד, "foundation") coalesces all the Divine forces that precede it into a singular creative impulse that constructively releases itself into reality. The purpose of this release is to fulfill the primal will of *keter*. The intervening *sefirot* through which that will passes on its way to *yesod* provide the essential logistical input that help one relate will to outer reality.

The term *yesod* is associated with the image of the *tzadik* ("righteous man"), as stated in the phrase[47] "the tzadik is the foundation of the universe." The tzadik represents the eminently expressive and influential creative-force that sustains and rectifies the material order. In *Sefer HaBahir*, the tzadik is referred to as a "pillar connecting heaven and earth." It is this pillar, firmly implanted in the ground of Creation, that comprises the very foundation of the universe.

The image of *yesod* as a link between heaven and earth is evoked in the verse designated in Kabbalah as the basis for naming the *sefirot*: "To You, O God, is the *gedulah* and the *gevurah* and the *tiferet* and the *netzach* and the *hod*, for all that is in heaven and earth is Yours..."[48] The words "for all" (כִּי כֹל, *ki chol*), appearing directly after the word *hod*, are equal in gematria to *yesod* (יְסוֹד, 80), the *sefirah* which actually follows *hod*. *Yesod* is repeatedly referred to in mystical sources as the force of totality (כֹּל, *kol*), insofar as it is the repository for all the sefirotic energy that precedes it as well as the channel for directing that energy into Creation and thereby bridging heaven and earth.[49]

In Kabbalah, *yesod* is often referred to as the "seal of truth," and indeed, the quality of **emet** (אֱמֶת, "truth"), its inner essence, best describes the way *yesod* expresses itself in the soul. By truth is meant the capacity, through one's active involvement in Creation, to produce a unique seal that bears testimony to the essential Divine character of one's soul and all reality.

The verification of one's own selfhood is the very essence of *yesod*. Whereas *netzach* and *hod* represent the promise of self-fulfillment, *yesod* brings that promise to fruition. It is the foundational power that enables one to conclude commitments to self and other, bound as one by a Divine oath of fidelity to God and His purpose in Creation.

As such, *yesod* is identified in Kabbalah with the reproductive organ, on which God chose to place the sign of His covenant (אוֹת בְּרִית קֹדֶשׁ, *ot brit kodesh*) with Israel. As the most potent instrument of human relationship, the fountain of man's procreative power, and—consequently—the measure of his moral responsibility to self and the world, the reproductive organ best symbolizes the character of *yesod*.

Together, the properties associated with *netzach*, *hod*, and *yesod* take the soul from an abstract reflective position, where the only movement it experiences is internally derived from the realm of intellect and emotion, and impel it toward concrete and active involvement with the world so as to verify its inner vision of reality. The *bitachon* of *netzach* begins the process by propelling the soul out of its inertial state, wherein it is content to merely think and feel, and into a mode whereby it braces itself for constructive action.

Together *netzach* and *hod* help one instinctively set a course that will lead to true creative fulfillment, the *temimut* of *hod* contributing constancy of vision and a persevering optimism. *Bitachon* continues working to assure that the momentum is accelerated so that the soul may advance toward the stage of final resolution, whereby the force of *emet* derived from *yesod* demands that one conclude the process and make one's creative impression upon the world.

Malchut

The final *sefirah*, **malchut** (מַלְכוּת, Divine "kingdom"), is understood in Kabbalah as expressive of God's implicit presence within the created order. Whereas the *sefirot* that precede it focus, each in their own way, upon the spirit of God influencing reality from above, the *sefirah* of *malchut* portrays that spirit as manifest within material Creation. For this reason, we find the *sefirah* of *malchut* symbolically identified in Kabbalah with the *Shechinah* (שְׁכִינָה, "the Divine Presence"), the relatively feminine representation of God[50] that is synonymous with His immanent spirit resting within Creation.

Malchut is the ground into which the full creative force of *yesod* is implanted. This force is absorbed by *malchut* and then converted into fuel for the perfection of material reality. The role of *malchut* in rectifying Creation necessitates two simultaneous yet contrasting postures on its part: one of supremacy, necessary for the enforcement of God's creative program, and one of humility, whereby the altruistic nature of one's attempt to influence and dominate the material realm becomes evident.

It is this posture of *shiflut* (שִׁפְלוּת, "lowliness"), the inner essence of *malchut*, that is expressed through God's lowering Himself, as it were, onto the throne of glory from which He directly oversees Creation.[51] From that vantage point, *malchut* proceeds to mandate order within the created realm by subjugating the proud and elevating the meek, intuitively maintaining proper balance and thereby fine-tuning Creation to perfection.

The quality of *shiflut* is what *malchut* inspires within the human soul. It is what enables one to act with kingly responsibility and devotion to the created realm. It guarantees that one's actions in life are motivated by the highest standards of justice and righteousness, unconcerned with personal gain or advantage. One who is a true king realizes that power is his not by individual right but by virtue of the responsibility to use the power with which he is blessed to help perfect reality.[52]

Notes:

1. Another way of explaining the differing emphases of Kabbalah and *Chasidut* is to say that Kabbalah focuses

on the *kelim* ("vessels") of Creation while *Chasidut* deals with the *orot* ("lights") that fill these vessels. This distinction is apparent even in the names attached to these two mystical traditions: The word "Kabbalah" (קבלה) is derived from the root קבל, which means, "to serve as a receptacle or vessel." The word "Chasidut" (חסידות) is constructed from the root חסד (*chesed*, "loving-kindness"), an attribute often referred to symbolically as the *"light* of day."

2. It is important to point out that according to this particular division, the number of inner powers in the soul (11) is equal to the number of all other properties combined (6 surrounding powers and 5 garments). This indicates that the eleven internal powers of the soul each reflect one of the remaining properties outside its native domain: the first six of these powers can be thought of as reflecting the six levels of the superconscious, while the remaining five imply the origin of the five garments.

   The 11 internal powers actually divide as well into 1 (the superconscious root of *chochmah*) and 10 (the remaining conscious powers). Consequently, the numbers 6, 11, and 5 end up corresponding to the letters ו, א, י and ה—the 4 vowel-characters in the 22-letter Hebrew alphabet which themselves are equal to 22 in *gematria*. The name of Jacob (יעקב), the archetypal soul of Israel and the twenty-second generation from Adam, is equal to 182—or the sum of 6^2, 11^2, and 5^2. (The separate sum of 1^2, 5^2, 6^2, and 10^2 equals 162, or

בצלם—"in the image" of God—hinting at the primordial creation of Adam whose soul was rectified through his counterpart, Jacob.)

3. Deuteronomy 4:4.

4. The element of anticipation which is common to both *emunah* and *ta'anug* (though directed at the diametrically opposed realities of this world and the World to Come) derives from their common association with the primal root of *keter, Atik Yomin*. As *the* primordial spiritual state, *Atik Yomin* implies the perennial anticipation of that which awaits the soul at the end of its journey through life.

   One of the three connotations attached to the Biblical root כתר is that of expectant waiting, as in Job 36:2: "Wait [כתר] for me a short while more and I will show you." (The other two meanings associated with the word *keter* in the Bible concur even more with its use as a symbol for superconscious experience: as a verb meaning to "encircle" and as a noun denoting a "crown.")

5. In Kabbalistic imagery, *shir* ("song") serves as a symbol of pleasure by virtue of its possessing the same geometric quality as does true pleasure, that of an ascending spiral (for otherwise, "continuous pleasure [i.e., pleasure which remains on a constant, non-ascending experiential plane] is not pleasure." The ascent is in the form a spiral, for pleasure, in general, is at the level of *keter*, whose basic meaning is "circle" [see previous footnote]. Not only does song [the natural,

spontaneous expression of the soul's experience of pleasure] possess the "circular" property of "its end being enwedged in its beginning," but one of the meanings of the word *shir* [שיר] itself is a [circular] "collar."). Consequently, the four levels of pleasure identified in *keter* are figuratively rendered in mystical texts as varying forms of musical harmony or counterpoint:

1. The *oneg pashut* of *emunah* is referred to as the *shir pashut* (שיר פשוט, "unstructured song"), while the three varieties of *oneg murkav* are referred to as:

2. the *shir kaful* (שיר כפול, "two-part song")— expressing harmony between the two powers of one's *sechel* (*chochmah* and *binah*);

3. the *shir meshulash* (שיר משולש, "three-part song")—expressing harmony between the three essential *midot* (*chesed*, *gevurah*, *tiferet*);

4. and the *shir meruba* (שיר מרובע, "four-part song")—expressing harmony between the four instinctive *midot* that culminate in rectified speech (*netzach*, *hod*, *yesod*, and *malchut*).

For a more complete treatment of this theme, see *Likutei Moharan Tinyana* 8 and *Torat Chaim, Bereishit*, p. 44.

6. The terms we have translated here as "supreme" and "common" (*elyon* and *tachton*, respectively) literally mean "higher" and "lower" and therefore also refer to

the respective positions these two varieties of will take relative to human reason—either above it (as in the will in *keter*) or below it, i.e. subservient to it (as in the will expressed through one's intellect) (See above, p. 59). We nevertheless chose to translate these terms as we have inasmuch as they reflect the varying styles of authority associated with will: the supreme will of the *keter* insists on exclusive rule, with no need for rational justification or support; the common will which accommodates one's intellect seeks to govern in accordance with revealed wisdom (as if to say that "common" will accommodates "common" sense).

7. Exodus 16:7.

8. Under closer inspection, we notice an interesting phenomenon at the juncture between superconscious will and conscious intellect: the lowest manifestation of will—common will—accords primarily with conscious reason, while the highest manifestation of one's intellect—the hidden intellect—is synonymous with the enlightening power of the superconscious.

 This sublime "handshake" between intellect and will (related to the "switching"-principle referred to in Kabbalah as אחליפו דוכתייהו) actually serves to link the opposing domains of the superconscious and the conscious in one's soul. Nonetheless, the essential origins of both the common will and the hidden intellect remain within their separate and indigenous realms— their apparent crossover expressing the complimentary reflection of each realm within the other.

9. This relationship is hinted at in Job 28:12: "and from where shall wisdom be found?" The word "from where" (מאין) can be read so as to imply: "and *chochmah* is found coming from *ayin*." It should also be noted that the term *ayin* is also employed to describe the intermediate realm of *keter*, the head of pleasure— which serves to arouse the *ko'ach hamaskil* to shoot its arrows of insight into revealed *chochmah*.

10. The intermediate level of *mal* is the channels that contract the infinite brilliance of the *ko'ach hamaskil* and direct its light-particles toward conscious *chochmah*. In Kabbalah, these channels are called the "hairs" of the "beard" (שערות הדיקנא) of the superconscious.

11. *Chagigah* 14a.

12. The relationship between joy and faith is evident as well in the association between the word אם (the joyous "mother") and אמונה ("faith"). Indeed, as explained numerous times in our books, just as the mother nurtures her child, faith nurtures the various powers of the soul. The idea of anticipating future life, conceptually binding these two roots together, is reflected as well in the Divine name of redemption identified in Kabbalah with *binah* and the power to give birth: the name אהי-ה, literally meaning "I will be(come)."

13. Together with the joy of the expectant mother during pregnancy (עיבור), comes a sense of trepidation and protectiveness, which often results in impatience or even anger (עברה) towards those around her. This

phenomenon is referred to in the *Zohar* (2:175b) as מינה דינין מתערין, "from her [i.e., *binah*] judgments arise."

14. See *Etz Chaim* 25b.

15. In certain Kabbalistic texts it is explained that *da'at* alludes to the outward manifestation of the Divine force to paradoxically bear opposites (here, the two opposites are in fact experienced as opposites which nonetheless coexist simultaneously), and is thus counted as one of the ten *sefirot* when their *outer* aspect is being considered. The deeper Chasidic understanding is the very opposite: *da'at* reflects the hidden essence of the paradoxical force (the experience of the two apparent opposites being, in essence, one and the same), and as such supplants *keter* when the *inner* aspect of the *sefirot* is being considered.

A figurative way of understanding the difference between *keter* and *da'at* would be to imagine as circular the opaque and impenetrable force-of-paradox that they both describe. *Keter* could be understood as perception of the circle's realm, as defined by its circumference alone, not tracing it back to its central point of origin. *Da'at*, on the other hand, could be thought of as the ability to perceive the inner parameters of this circle—its center and radius—and thereby provide consciousness with the inner coordinates required for exploring the mystery that inheres within it.

16. The *sefirot* are depicted in Kabbalah as being arranged along three axes: the right axis is associated with the

expansive, revelatory properties of *chochmah, chesed,* and *netzach*; the left axis with the constraining, concealing properties of *binah, gevurah,* and *hod*; and the central axis with the integrative properties of *da'at, tiferet, yesod,* and *malchut. Da'at* is unique insofar as it integrates not only the horizontally-aligned powers of *chochmah* and *binah* immediately above it, but also the vertically-aligned domains of intellect and character attributes between which it is poised.

The role *da'at* plays in uniting the forces of *chochmah* and *binah* is referred to in the Kabbalah as *da'at elyon* (דעת עליון, "higher *da'at*"), while its function as a bridge between the intellect and the emotions is referred to as *da'at tachton* (דעת תחתון, "lower *da'at*") (See *Tanya, Igeret HaKodesh* 15, end). This terminology is meant to express the relative position of these two states in the hierarchy of conscious experience, rather than their respective importance as a whole (see p. 76).

The *da'at* binding *chochmah* and *binah* together is also referred to in Kabbalah as *da'at hane'elam* (דעת הנעלם, "hidden *da'at*") whereas the *da'at* giving birth to and sustaining one's emotions is called *da'at hamitpashet* (דעת המתפשט, "extending *da'at*"). The identification of two states of *da'at* is derived from I Samuel 2:3, which describes God as possessing two levels of knowledge.

17. Genesis 4:6.

18. These two effects in the realm of human consciousness actually reflect differing aspects of the Divine unification between *chochmah* and *binah*: the outer-

unification of these two *sefirot* is what enables God to sustain created being as it already exists, a process referred to as חדוש העולמות, "the ongoing renewal of Creation." The inner unification of these two *sefirot* accomplishes the even more mysterious feat of introducing altogether new and unprecedented spiritual energy into Creation, which is called הולדת נשמות חדשות, "birthing new souls."

19. This function of *da'at* is expressed through the statement of the *Zohar* which refers to it as "the key to [opening] the six [chambers of the heart]," i.e., the emotive properties of the soul. The portrayal of the *midot* as chambers or rooms of the heart is alluded to in Proverbs 24:4: "And by *da'at* are chambers filled" — whereby the word for "chamber," חדר, serves as an acronym for *chesed* (חסד), *din* (דין, synonymous with *gevurah*), and *rachamim* (רחמים), the three axes (right, left, and middle, respectively) of emotive life.

Da'at is able to harmonize the two most diametrically opposed elements of the affective realm — *chesed* and *gevurah*, love and fear — by virtue of its possessing five forces of *chesed* (powers of attraction) and five forces of *gevurah* (powers of constriction), paralleling the full array of the soul's ten powers. In *Sefer Yetzirah*, we find the ten *sefirot* as referring to the five fingers of the right hand (*chesed*) and the five fingers of the left hand (*gevurah*). Later Kabbalistic texts interpret this to mean that the five fingers of the right hand reflect, on the physical plane, the five *sefirot* of *keter*, *chochmah*, *chesed*, *tiferet* and *netzach*, which tend to the right (on the spiritual plane), and that the five fingers of the left hand reflect the five *sefirot* of *binah, gevurah, hod, yesod* and *malchut,* which tend to the left. The Arizal explains that the five fingers of the right hand are in fact the final, physical manifestation of the five forces of *chesed* contained within *da'at,* whereas the five fingers of the left hand are the final, physical manifestation of the five forces of *gevurah* contained within it. The harmony of the two hands working in conjunction (as symbolized by all ten fingers playing together a musical instrument) is an expression of one's inner faculty of *da'at.*

20. In the terminology of Kabbalah, the relationship between emotion and the superconscious is formulated as זו"א בעתיקא אחיד ותליא, "the minor realm [i.e., that of the *midot*] is bound up with the Ancient One [the primordial *keter*]."

21. The presence of *da'at* within the *midot* (as is the case regarding the presence of *keter* as well) is likened to that of lights within vessels, or a soul within a body. When *da'at* actively asserts itself within the context of a particular *midah,* the result is an emotive experience that radiates with Divine significance—such as the love or fear of God. When *da'at* removes itself from that *midah,* an impression of light still remains imprinted upon its exterior—allowing for the sustained appearance of refinement we have identified as one's second nature (*teva sheni*).

22. Thus indicating that one's *da'at* is not sufficiently strong; one's soul not sufficiently mature.

23. See for instance Genesis 6:8.

24. See for instance Esther 2:15. The verb "to carry" implies the ability "to bear opposites" (נשיאת הפכים), i.e., to sustain a paradoxical state of unity.

25. See in length in our Hebrew volume, *Machol Hakrameem*, especially chapter 4.

26. The corresponding term applicable to the properties of one's intellect is *muskal* (מושכל, "reasoned").

27. See *Body, Mind, and Soul*, p. 24.

28. *Da'at* is in fact referred to as the soul of the emotions (נשמת ז"א).

29. 89:3.

30. Hence, the word חסד hints at the words חס דלית, "compassion for he who has naught."

31. The reference to *chesed* as *gedulah* is based upon I Chronicles 29:11, from which the names and order of the seven lower *sefirot* are derived: "To You, O God, is the *gedulah* and the *gevurah* and the *tiferet*…"

32. This function of *chesed* is reflected in its depiction by the *Zohar* as the "day of Creation accompanying all other days" (the seven lower *sefirot* are commonly identified in Kabbalah with the seven days of Creation), an association inspired by Psalms 42:9: "God will command His *chesed* day by day."

33. Michah 7:20.

34. Isaiah 41:8.

35. Joshua 14:15.

36. The two words גבורה and יראה both equal 216 in *gematria*.

37. See *The Art of Education*, pp. 244ff.

38. This quality is evident as well in the concept of מחלוקת לשם שמים ("argument for the sake of heaven"), wherein antithetical positions are seen as capable of coexisting so along as they jointly acknowledge the Divine force of *tiferet* harmonizing them at their root.

39. Of the four powers distributed along the central axis of the *sefirot*, *da'at* and *tiferet* are said to tend toward the right while *yesod* and *malchut* tend toward the left (see above, footnote 19).

    The ability of *rachamim* to overpower *yirah* in line with its innate disposition toward *ahavah* is reflected in the Scriptural expression (Isaiah 29:22): "Jacob, who has redeemed Abraham." Jacob, identified in Kabbalah as the symbol of *tiferet*, possesses the power to redeem Abraham—the model of *chesed*—from the grips of *gevurah*. See *Tanya*, chapter 32.

40. הבטחה, from the same root as בטחון.

41. As in Deuteronomy 8:18: "And remember GOD your God, for *He* grants you the power to succeed."

42. The *sefirah* of *hod* represents the other kidney, or companion counsel, joining *netzach* in the advance of the soul.

43. The very name "Jew" (יהודי) derives from הוד and thus indicates that the most essential manifestation of one's

Jewishness is the ability of the Jew to acknowledge, fully, in truth, that God our Creator is the unique, supreme power and infinite source of intelligence to Whom we bow.

44. It is this second connotation that draws *hod* into association with the *sefirot* of *keter* and *malchut* (kingdom), all three expressing properties of majesty. Of the identified names for the *sefirot*, *keter* and *hod* are the only two that appear in Scripture in construct form with the word *malchut*, i.e. "*keter malchut*" and "*hod malchut*." In addition, the word *hod* (הוד) comprises the root of the name *Yehudah* (יהודה) — the ancestral figure of kingship (*malchut*) in Israel, David's chief progenitor.

In fact, the name David (דוד) — the archetype soul of *malchut* — is comprised of three letters which are virtually identical to those in the word *hod*, differing only by the small jot that distinguishes the *hei* in *hod* from the first *dalet* in David. In *gematria*, the two words differ by the mere value of one. David, equal to 14, was the fourteenth generation descended from our father Abraham. His son Solomon, who is described in I Chronicles 29:25 as unequaled in his embodiment of *hod malchut*, was the fifteenth generation from Abraham — 15 being the *gematria* of *hod*.

King Solomon's ascent to power, the high point of our national history, is often rendered figuratively as the image of the moon — symbol of Israel — achieving its fullest light on the fifteenth day of its monthly cycle.

The reduced value of the name "Solomon" (שלמה) is actually equal to 15.

45. Jeremiah 31:3.

46. Proverbs 10:9.

47. Ibid. 10:25.

48. I Chronicles 29:11.

49. As a channel linking heaven and earth, *yesod* is re-enacting at a more advanced level the role of *da'at*, poised between one's intellect and character attributes, seeking a balance between abstraction and expressiveness.

50. *Malchut* is also referred to in Kabbalah as *nukva* (נוקבא, "the female"), *bat* (בת, "the daughter"), *malkah* (מלכה, "the queen") or *ima tata'ah* (אמא תתאה, "the lower mother," as opposed to *binah*, the "higher mother").

51. The throne symbolizes the seemingly untenable capacity to assert authority while lowered into a position of equal par with one's subjects.

52. The *sefirah* of *malchut* is characterized in Kabbalah as "possessing nothing of her own" (*Zohar*, 2:215a). King David, the quintessential figure of kingdom, declares in II Samuel 6:24: "lowly shall I be in my own eyes," expressing the state of *shiflut* that occupies the core of his kingly consciousness.

7

Structural Analysis

Structural Analysis 7

Now that we have explored the "Tree of Life" — the Jewish soul — from its deepest roots to its outermost branch, let us consider some significant aspects of its overall structure.

The various branches of the Jewish soul ultimately amount to twenty-two[1] distinct manifestations of our unique capacity to will, apprehend, feel, and act in accord with the singular Divine purpose etched into our being. Implicit in these twenty-two properties are thirteen specific measures-of-experience emanating from the seven major branches of powers and garments: pleasure, will, intellect, character attributes, thought, speech, and action.

Let us now consider the mathematical structure of our tree as represented by the number of components at each level of its hierarchy.

As is evident in our diagram, on its way to achieving full conceptual articulation, the soul passes through five separate divisions. Numerically, the divisions define a progression from 1 to 2 to 3 to 7 to 13 to 22 individual distinctions in the soul. Let us then look at this numerical series—1, 2, 3, 7, 13, 22—and see the meaningful patterns that it reflects.

The first thing we notice is that the sum of the first 5 numbers, 1, 2, 3, 7, and 13 is 26, the numerical value of God's essential Name, *Havayah* (י־הוה). Interestingly, with the last number, 22, the series alludes to the Hebrew word for כוכב, which means "star." The first two letters of this word, כו, equal 26 and the final two letters, כב, equal 22.

The next phenomenon that becomes apparent is the relationship possessed by both the pair 2 and 3 as well as 7 and 13: the first number in each of these pairs is the mid-point of its partner (2 is the mid-point of 3, and 7 of 13. In general, n is the mid-point of 2n – 1. Concomitantly, the first number in the series—the indivisible 1—is in fact the mid-point of itself. Hence, was this pattern to continue, the next pair of numbers to follow in the series would demonstrate the same relationship.

We have already identified the first number in that pair—22. The next number of our algebraic series can be derived by performing a simple algorithm called finite differences, as follows:

Let us first arrange our set of numbers alongside one another:

$$1 \qquad 2 \qquad 3 \qquad 7 \qquad 13 \qquad 22$$

Now, underneath them, let us write the numerical difference between each progressive pair of integers:

1		2		3		7		13		22
	1		1		4		6		9	

Let us now repeat this same process for each descending line of numbers:

1		2		3		7		13		22
	1		1		4		6		9	
		0		3		2		3		
			3		-1		1			
				-4		2				
					6					

Now, in order to derive the next number in our initial series, we must add the base of the entire structure (6) to the last number in the series above it (2) and continue in this fashion—adding the new number to the final one in each ascending series—until we arrive at the next integer in our initial progression.

1		2		3		7		13		22		43
	1		1		4		6		9		21	
		0		3		2		3		12		
			3		-1		1		9			
				-4		2		8				
					6		6					

As can be seen, the next number in the series, 43, does indeed bear out the pattern that we had expected, being as its paired number, 22, is also its mid-point.

By repeating the above procedure again and again, we generate the following succession of numbers:

1   2   3   7   13   22   43   99   233   514   1043   ...

The specific pattern that we uncovered in the first seven numbers of our series appears to end with the number 43. By adding all the seven integers from 1 to 43, we arrive at the sum 91, which is the numerical value of the word אִילָן (ilan), meaning "tree."

The ninth number of our series reflects an even more amazing association: 233 is the value of עֵץ הַחַיִּים (Etz Hacha'im), meaning, "the Tree of Life," the focus of our study. 233 is also the 13th number in the Fibonacci series (or the series of love numbers, as it is referred to in Kabbalah). Adding to all of the above, we now note that the sum of 13, 22, 43, and 99—the four numbers preceding 233—is 177, which is also the numerical value of גַּן עֵדֶן (Gan Eden), "the Garden of Eden." Indeed, the Torah tells us that the Tree of Life was situated at the exact mid-point of the Garden of Eden (as indicated by the verse, "And the Tree of Life was in the middle of the garden").

The number 91—once again, the sum of the first seven integers in our above series—elicits many other meaningful associations: Firstly, it hints at the unification of God's two Names—God's essential Name, Havayah (יהוה), which equals and the Name אדנ־י, whose value is 65. The first of these two Names is equal to the sum of the first 5 integers in our progression (1, 2, 3, 7, and 13); the second name is equal to the sum of the remaining two integers (22 and 43). This arrangement of integers—7 broken into a group of 5 and a group of 2—hints at the fashion in which the seven candles of the Menorah in the Holy Temple were daily prepared for lighting, first 5 candles and then, later in the morning, the remaining 2. The numbers 7, 5, and 2 in fact correspond to the letters *zayin* (ז), *hei* (ה), and *beit* (ב), which together spell זָהָב (*zahav*), "gold," the metal from which the menorah was constructed. This correlation between the image of the menorah and that of the *Etz Hacha'im* reflects their common use in Midrashic lore as symbols of the Torah.

Perhaps most meaningfully in terms of the hierarchy of our "tree," the number 91 is the product of its two prime factors: 7 and 13, the numbers that correspond to the major branches of experience identified on our diagram.[2] Consequently, the seven hierarchic levels of our tree each possess an average value of 13, indicating that the 13 measures of experience delineated above comprise a core terminology for understanding the entire structure of the soul.

All that remains for us now is to explain the conceptual significance of the number 43, the final number of branches ascribed to our tree according to the numerical pattern identified above. An obvious way of explaining the significance of the number 43 relative to the prior level of 22 would be to once again suggest that every property or function of the soul "split" in two—aside from the garment of action, which we have repeatedly indicated retains a unitary character.

The dual aspect associated with the first 21 properties can be understood in terms of the fundamental Chasidic principle regarding the dual-character of Creation referred to in Ecclesiastes 7:14 as *zeh le'umat zeh* (זֶה לְעֻמַּת זֶה, "the one opposite the other"). Indeed, 43 is also the value of the word גַּם, meaning "also," another way of indicating the duality of this and that. The expression *zeh le'umat zeh* is employed in *Chasidut* to indicate that both the holy and the mundane within Creation derive from a common Divine source. This is to say that every force God has planted within the universe can be used in either of two ways, for the sanctification of God's Name or for the mundane edification of self. Drawing their inspiration from a common creative force, these two inverse pursuits can often share a similar character, differing only in intention and effect.

As regards the realm of the soul, the principle of *zeh le'umat zeh* is reflected in the Chasidic doctrine whereby we are taught that the Jew possesses a separate *nefesh Elokit* (נֶפֶשׁ אֱלֹקִית, "Divine soul") and *nefesh bahamit* (נֶפֶשׁ בַּהֲמִית, "animal soul"). The *nefesh bahamit* represents a specific configuration of internal forces promoting an identification between the self and material Creation. The *nefesh Elokit*, with an infinitely higher source in Divinity, cultivates an identification in the opposite direction—toward the world's Divine point of origin.

Consequently, the dual-aspect which we have inferred with regard to the above 21 properties can be thought of as reflecting the contrasting identifications of the animal and Divine souls, producing a total of 42 manifestations in the Jewish soul. The garment of action, which we have described as essentially neutral and beyond the dichotomies imposed upon it from without, contributes the final element completing the full set of 43 properties in the soul.

Notes:

1. The obvious significance of the number 22 is that it represents the number of letters in the Hebrew alphabet. Each letter can be thought of as a code for

representing one of the soul's unique properties.

The basic division of the soul's anatomy into 17 powers and 5 garments alludes to the masculine and feminine forms of the word טוב (meaning, "good") in Hebrew. The value of טוב (the masculine form) is 17, and with an additional letter *hei* (ה) whose value is 5, it becomes טובה, the feminine form (whose value is 22). These two numbers also allude to the two Kabbalistic Names of God that correspond to the male and female aspect of *da'at*: אהוה = טוב = 17, corresponds to the male aspect and טובה = אהוי = 22, corresponds to the female aspect.

Furthermore, the sum of 17^2 and 5^2 is 314, the numerical value of the holy Name, שדי (pronounced, *Shakai*), which corresponds to the *sefirah* of *yesod*.

The sums of the triangles of each letter of the feminine form of "good," טובה is 45 ⊥ 21 ⊥ 3 ⊥ 15 = 84, which in Kabbalah is associated with the rectification of the covenant of the *sefirah* of *yesod*. The sum of the triangles of 17 and 5 is 168, twice the value of 84, indicating a relation of 1:2, a ratio known in Kabbalah as "a whole and a half."

2. The sub-factors of 91 associated above with two primary Names of God—26 (*Yud-Kei-Vav-Kei*) and 65 (*Alef-Dalet-Nun-Yud*)—are each a multiple of 13 as well: the number 26 is equal to 13 times 2 (the number of integers from our initial series whose sum is 65) while 65 is equal to 13 times 5 (the number of integers whose sum is 26)—thus reflecting the unification of these two Names at an even deeper level.

Subject Index

Bibliographic Index

Proper Names Index

Gematria Index

www.ingramcontent.com/pod-product-compliance
Lightning Source LLC
Chambersburg PA
CBHW020214290326
41948CB00001B/45